Digging Your Own Well:

Daoism as a Practical Philosophy

By Cloudwalking Owl (Bill Hulet)

Cloudwalking Books

2016

First printing 2016

ISBN 978-0-9938395-3-5

Cloudwalking Books

124-A Surrey St. East

Guelph, Ontario, Canada

N1H 3P9

thecloudwalkingowl@gmail.com

To my sweet lovely partner Misha

You inspire me with your courage

and support me more than anyone else in my life

Who am I?

I'm not some ancient Chinese sage. Instead, I'm a white Canadian who is past middle-age moving towards being a senior citizen. I don't know any oriental languages. I've never lived in or even visited China. I'm not even a scholar of anything Chinese. I have a Master's degree in philosophy, but I have worked for about thirty years as a porter in an academic library. Nothing about that would give anyone a reason to read my book about Daoism.

Well, there is other stuff too. Many years ago I decided that I was out of shape and should follow an exercise regime. I thought martial arts were cool, so I looked around for one. I had never heard about this thing called "taijiquan", but there was a club in town and it looked like something I could do to get more fit. Maybe later on I'd switch to something better, like tae kwon do or karate. It turned out that taijiquan was more interesting than I had thought. There were a very interesting bunch of people involved with the club and I started hanging out with them. Eventually I ended up going with them to events at the school's "head office" in Toronto.

There I met the founder. He was a strange immigrant from China who didn't speak a word of English. He did bizarre things like insisting on sleeping on the floor of the studio with a telephone book as a pillow. He also liked to eat and would often ask us to go out after classes for meals. I'm a bit of "joiner" and I eventually volunteered to do some stuff for the organization.

One day this guy---Moy Lin Shin---asked me (through a translator) if I'd like to "join the Temple". I asked what it involved and the first thing he said was "well, for starts, it costs $300 to join". That stopped things for me right there. I said "well, it might be a good idea but there's absolutely no way I can afford that". (At the time I was working as a janitor for minimum wage.) Next week he came to me again "if you want to join the Temple, there's a 'special introductory offer'. You can join for $30". I thought "what's there to lose?" Eventually I got ushered into this hot little Daoist Temple that had been built into an apartment in the heart of Toronto (the Fung Loy

Kok), told to wear some very heavy robes over my street clothes, and went through this elaborate ceremony that involved me kow-towing in front of an altar and offering three splints of wooden incense on a brazier.

I did some other stuff for the school and spent a summer helping out as a live-in volunteer at a retreat centre in Orangeville. But eventually I found myself in the middle of some very strange inter-personal dynamics in the organization and decided that I was no longer interested in the Taoist Tai Chi Association of Canada.

Then something very interesting happened. After I left Mr. Moy went kinda berzerk. I was told that he sent telegrams (yes, they still existed back then) all over the world saying that I was "persona non-grata". That struck me as totally bizarre because I really wasn't that important to the taiji school or the temple. It was only many years later that I found out why he flipped out.

....

I came across this group called "the Taoist Restoration Society". It was a non-profit that was trying to help preserve and restore Daoism in China. It had the support of quite a few scholars and a very impressive website. One of the features that they had was an "ask an expert" question and answer forum. One day someone asked an expert how one would go about being "baptised" as a Daoist. The professor said that that was impossible as Daoism is an elitist religion that doesn't have "followers" like members of a Christian church. Instead, it is more like what we in the West would know as a monastic order. At that point, I stepped in and describe the ceremony I'd gone through and asked what that was if it wasn't something like a Christian baptism. The academic responded by saying that that hadn't been a "baptism", instead it had been an "ordination".

I was dumbfounded.

Later on, I connected on line with a scholar of religious studies who was researching the Fung Loy Kok Temple. When I explained my background to him, he got very excited and eventually travelled to my home to interview me about my experience. He told me that Mr. Moy had only asked a very small number of people to "join the temple" and that it was extremely rare for anyone---let alone a

Westerner with no Chinese---to go through that ceremony at any Temple in any country. I literally had had no clue about this. It explained why Moy had reacted so explosively to my defection.

Well, that's a cool story, but so what? Not much. But there are other things. A strange thing about my defection from the Taoist Tai Chi Association was that I ended up sticking with the practices that I learned there. I kept up the regular taijiquan practice. I pursued various meditation techniques for decades. I went to workshops from other schools and learned stuff like the Yang sword routine. I even joined the Canadian Taijiquan Federation for a while and went to events when possible. I also spent time trying to learn from non-Daoists. I had a Roman Catholic hermit as a spiritual director for years. I've also gone to Zen meditation retreats, classes inspired by other Buddhist traditions and so on. I've also spent a lot of time studying books about Daoism. I happen to have a Master's degree in philosophy which allows me to use some of the academic "tricks of the trade" to try and learn as much as possible. Working at an academic library and having access to the Internet haven't hurt either.

It wasn't that I really thought of myself as a Daoist through most of this period. Indeed, I was more interested in Buddhism or Sufism. I even seriously contemplated becoming a Roman Catholic. (I gagged at a class for potential converts that exposed me to what "popular Catholicism" really looks like.) I did "sign the book" and become a Unitarian---but I eventually drifted away from that too. There always seemed to be something keeping me from completely integrating into these systems of thought and communities of believers. So when I found out about my "ordination", I decided that I might as well hang my hat on that hook as any other.

I recall reading somewhere (although I've never been able to see that reference again) that there is a custom among some Daoists to follow a practice called "cloud walking". This involved travelling from temple to temple in order to learn from the different communities in China. In fact, the temples didn't even have to be Daoist, as it was assumed that "all religions are one" and that there was much a person could learn from studying with Buddhists and even Christians and Muslims. Since I have spent my life trying to learn from any number of different spiritual traditions, I see myself as someone who has spent decades "cloudwalking". And because my last name, Hulet, is supposed to mean "member of the Owl Clan" in old Welsh (at least by family tradition), I have taken on the Daoist name of "the Cloudwalking Owl".[1]

If that little snippet of an autobiography peaks your interest, then maybe you should go on and finish the rest of the book.

Why Should You Read this Book?

There are a significant number of people who describe themselves as "spiritual but not religious". These are folks who do not want to live a life of materialist consumption. They believe that "Whoever has the most toys when they die wins" isn't much of a way to live a life.

At the same time, the religious institutions that purport to be the arbiters of all value in our society seem positively unhinged. Setting aside the most odious examples of abuse of power---such as the sexual abuse of children or using ministries as mechanisms for amassing personal wealth---most mainstream churches have emphasized the trivial and ignored the substantial. Religious organizations seem to be totally obsessed with sex. Any sort of expansion of civil rights for homosexuals and transgenders is abhorred and abortion is considered a form of murder. Thoughtful people find this emphasis bizarre. They often know people with non-traditional sexual orientation and don't understand why they are to be so feared. And anyone with a passing knowledge of biology can't understand why a world that is so profoundly profligate with life would be concerned about whether or not a fertilized human egg fulfills its potential and becomes a baby.

In contrast, anyone with eyes to see notices the existential threat of climate change. They also see the tremendous imbalance of wealth that neo-liberalism has caused. A small percentage of people have much more than they need---and many more others have to struggle

---

1 People who know something about Daoist naming systems might bridle at my taking on this name. Traditionally lineages have a "name poem" and people's religious names are assigned sequentially from the words in it. That means that anyone in that lineage can hear a person's name, look up the poem, and tell which person has seniority over any other. The organization that Moy came from, the Yuen-Yuen Institute in Hong Kong, doesn't follow that system. It is more of a "reformed" type of Daoism. It was formed by refugee Daoists who fled because of Communist persecution. Since these refugees had come from lots of different schools, sticking to a lineage poem system made no sense and it was discarded.

just to survive. Our governments are also engaged in endless "low-intensity" wars that only affect a few brutalized veterans here, but spread misery to untold millions in other nations.

People see these problems and cannot understand why what seems to be the loudest, most self-confident, and, most influential religious institutions fixate upon sexual orientation and abortion while ignoring the mountain of injustice and misery that surrounds us. It is true that there are many religious groups doing great work. The civil rights movement in the sixties, for example, was sustained by the black community's churches. Without the enormous amount of "street level" ministry that many religious institutions offer, many poor and destitute people would have nowhere to turn. But for all that is good with some religious institutions, this isn't enough to overcome the bad that many people see coming from religious groups' bizarre definition of what is and is not of ultimate value to human beings.

A large part of the problem is that the world that traditional religion springs from is profoundly at odds with the day-to-day life of most people. The political vision embodied in Abrahamic religions[2] is rigidly hierarchical, patriarchal, and authoritarian. God is an absolute dictator who enforces his laws through the use of an eternal concentration camp known as "Hell". Modern people inhabit democracies where leadership is through consensus building and power flows from the bottom up instead of the top down. Free expression is encouraged---not only as a human right, but also because truth is seem as flowing from a conversation between equals who each bring their own personal viewpoint to a complex issue. Science---who's amazing insights and creations we take for granted---is also based on the free flow of ideas and argument over competing hypotheses.

This divergence between the religious worldview and the modern life experience is probably best summed up by way religious conservatives view hypocrisy. Modernists view it as a deadly sin, because it allows individuals experiencing cognitive dissonance to avoid reassessing their cherished beliefs. If a priest simply cannot follow his vow of celibacy, for example, the experience gives him a chance to rethink his definition of what it means to be a human being.

---

2 Judaism, Christianity, and, Islam.

Perhaps we are not spiritual souls trapped in flesh who have total control over our behaviour in all situations. Instead, maybe we are products of evolution who have very strong instinctual drives that need to be accepted and integrated into life. The honest man can work through this calculus and change his life. In contrast, the hypocrite dismisses the cognitive dissonance as an example of "the spirit is willing but the flesh is weak". From the "inside out" this feels like an example of humility by a "fallen human being", but from the outside it seems like a lack of moral courage and duplicity.

In contrast, conservative religious people believe that the greatest sin is rebellion. That was the sin of Satan, after all. Yet the problem with this is that so many of our most cherished institutions are the result of rebellion. The USA was founded by a rebellion. The parliamentary democracy that it rebelled against was itself the product of an earlier, English rebellion against an absolutist monarch. The computer that I am writing this book on is itself a product of several scientific "rebellions" against an old way of thinking. It is obvious to anyone with eyes to see that rebellion is not an isolated act of will, but rather one of the key agents of human progress. If people have to choose between hypocrisy and rebellion, the forward-looking, clear-eyed, honest people of today will choose rebellion every time.

I have written this book to help people understand that it is possible to develop and pursue a life of value without turning your back on reason and personal experience. In my own case, the values that I have adopted are Daoist. There are other options out there too. This is the way of non-religious values. They are provisional. What this means is that they are always open to debate, and if in that conversation someone is able to convince you that one of your beliefs is not supported by either reason or experience, then you should be willing to change it. This may---and in practical terms does---mean that there are different sets of plausible values besides the ones that work for me. Other people have different life experiences that lead them to see things differently. It might be that there ultimately is only one really coherent set of values, but the fact is that if there is, none of us have the time and energy to figure them out. We all live a short life and have only limited opportunities. Maybe our culture will slowly and painstakingly work itself closer and closer to this ultimate set of values---but that's not going to happen in my lifetime. So we must pay our money and make our choice. This book explains my choice and invites others to make their own.

Practical Philosophy

In modern times "philosophy" has become a purely academic pursuit. Professors at universities write papers for each other where they discuss very abstract concepts. I'm not going to say that this is a totally worthless pursuit, as some of the ideas that they develop end up becoming extremely important for science, literature, politics, and so on. Human society cannot evolve without creating new ways of thinking about the world, and someone has to do it.

But philosophy used to also be about how to live a life of meaning and purpose. In the late Roman Empire there were schools of philosophy that helped ordinary people. The most famous were Stoicism, Cynicism, and Skepticism. Each of these were systemic ways of looking at and living in the world. They allowed followers to find meaning and coherence in turbulent times. Unfortunately, they were suppressed by the Christian church once it became the official--- and exclusive---religion of the Roman Empire. Philosophy continued in academic settings, but it was never again allowed to escape into the lives of ordinary citizens.

At roughly the same time, philosophy also arose in India and China. India's most famous examples are Yoga and Buddhism. In China, some examples were Confucianism, Moism, Daoism, and Legalism. In India it's practical philosophies became overlaid by religious thinking to the point where for most people their original teachings pretty much disappeared. In China this also happened to Daoism. Confucianism continued to exist as a practical way of life, but it became entwined with the Imperial bureaucracy, which stopped innovation in its tracks---making it more of an official ideology than a living, breathing philosophy. Moism (a socialist/utilitarian/scientific worldview) was effectively exterminated after its followers lost a literal war with Legalism (a totalitarian worldview based on the rigid rule of law.) Legalism's success at founding the first Chinese Empire proved a Pyrrhic victory, though, because it's extremely harsh treatment of ordinary people resulted in rebellions that quickly destroyed that dynasty and its governing philosophy. Confucianism reasserted itself as the dominant school and defined what it means to be "Chinese" for millennia afterwards.

(Of course, this is all a grotesque over-simplification, but people have to start somewhere and this book is not an academic historical treatise.)

....

OK. There was this thing in the past. Why should anyone care today?

When I was a child one of my teachers used to write sayings on the blackboard every morning. One that stuck out in my mind was "Be a live wire and you won't get stepped on!". At the time, I thought that it meant that people shouldn't be afraid of standing up for their rights, asserting their interests, or, showing off their abilities. It struck me as an advertisement in favour of the value of being "pushy". As a child, I thought that this was a bit odd, as my family had always taught me that that was being rude.

Why did that teacher write it on the black board?

Totally unconsciously, she was promoting a "practical philosophy". In particular, she was promoting a sort of optimistic, liberal, 20th century view of "individual progress". Contrast that with this similar piece of folk wisdom: "The nail that sticks out shall be hammered down." That is a Japanese proverb that seems to suggest that it is dangerous to be a "live wire". Not only will being "live" not keep you from being "stepped on"---it will positively ensure that you will be.

Which one is right?

Well, that's an important question because depending on how you choose, you will live your life in a particular way and either reap the benefits or suffer the consequences. The practical philosophies that I mentioned above---Greek, Indian, and, Chinese---are all coherent collections of ideas about how you should live your life. They all suggest that it is better to follow an internally consistent series of maxims instead of simply bouncing through life following whatever random ideas your culture (eg my elementary school teacher) chooses

12

to insert into your consciousness. This book is an attempt to expose the reader to one of those schools of practical philosophy: Daoism. My hope is that some of you will see the great wisdom that I have found that it brought to my life, and how it helps me navigate the day-to-day problems that I face.

And in the case of that maxim that my home room teacher wrote on the black board, a Daoist would probably have written "Be like water". That is, find effective "work-arounds" for life's problems instead of either vainly fighting against impossible odds or just doing what everyone else does.

Spelling

Some folks who read this book are going to be surprised by the way I spell a lot of words. For example, most books write "tai chi chuan" instead of "taijiquan", "Taoism" instead of "Daoism", "Lao Tsu" instead of "Laozi", "Chuang Tsu" instead of "Zhuangzi", and so on. What I am doing is using a modern, official method of transliterating Chinese words called "pinyin" instead of an older system that was invented by Western missionaries and academics. The reason why I use it is because it's the way the Chinese government wants us to spell it. Since China has been horribly "screwed over" by Western imperialists for a very, very long time. I think it's only polite to spell their language the way they want.

....

Generally Western books about Daoism follow a 19th century transliteration system call "Wade-Giles". (This is the "tai chi chuan", "Taoism", etc.) But it was replaced by the new pinyin system in the late 20th century. This is not just an arcane issue for translators, though. Written Chinese is very different from Western languages in that it is not based on sounds but ideas. This means that anyone trying to learn how to read and write in Chinese doesn't have the option of "spelling out" the letters of a word and then using the sounds to figure out its meaning. For hundreds of years educated Chinese people have understood how the use of letters instead of picture-graphs makes it much, much easier to learn. But traditional Chinese has one huge advantage over Western letters: it allows people who speak different dialects to use the same written language. Ancient Latin mutated into several different languages: Italian, French, Spanish, Portuguese, and so on. Chinese did the same thing: Mandarin, Hakka, Yue (Cantonese), Jin, and so on. Now people who read and write French cannot understand oral or written Portuguese because both are based on the sound of the spoken language. But in China, people who only speak Hakka and others who only understand Mandarin can read what each other writes---because the language is based on ideas and pictures instead of sound.

Since traditionally only a small percentage of Chinese citizens were literate, the extreme difficulty of learning the language wasn't considered a big problem. And the huge size of China almost guaranteed that any attempt to create a standardized spoken language would be doomed to fail. The ability of the written language to transcend the emergence of dialects was a tremendous asset when it came to keeping the nation from falling to pieces (like the Roman Empire did in Europe.) To a large extend, the "idiosyncrasies" of written Chinese allowed the nation to survive.

But now is now and China needs universal literacy if it is going to function in the modern world. So the government embarked on the very ambitious project of making Mandarin the standard language. And once people learned that, it allowed them to make learning written Chinese much easier. That is, it is easier to teach adult learners the European letters, then the pinyin spelling for each of the common characters that ordinary people use, and, then learn the characters associated with that pinyin. Pinyin also is important in being able to use various modern technologies such as computer keyboards. (Try to imagine using a keyboard that worked using traditional characters----!) This means that European letters are now integral to using Chinese in various settings. As a result, all children in mainland China are now taught pinyin as part of their elementary school education.

What this means is that pinyin is not just a transliteration system for Westerners, it is now a basic part of the Chinese language. And as such, using the old Wade-Giles transliterations is not only insulting, but quite wrong. This is also why I try to use pinyin instead.

If anyone wants to learn about Daoism by reading texts---and this is pretty much essential unless you want to learn Mandarin and move to the Wudang Mountains (the Daoist equivalent of Shaolin Temple)---it is essential that the reader prepare herself for the experience. Most Western books attempt to clearly explain issues using precise language. That is to say, they usually attempt to create "recipes": 'add two cups of flour to one egg plus one cup of milk and then bake at 300 degrees for thirty minutes'. In contrast, books on Daoism are metaphorical and lyrical: 'Master Li rode the phoenix and ascended to the mountains'. Another way of saying this is to generalize and say that Western books tend to be explicit and Daoist ones are evocative.

Explicit literature is designed to standardize a particular process. If you want to bake a specific type of cake, you have to know exactly what ingredients in what amounts are to be treated in a specific way. Being a Daoist is not like baking a cake, however. It isn't about standardization, instead it is about a particular person in a particular situation realizing his particular potential. An author cannot do this for a reader. All he can attempt to do is get her thinking.

....

I spent a summer at a Daoist retreat centre. The high teacher was rarely there, but one day he was and came through the kitchen just as I was drinking a glass of water. Through his translator he told me a story from when he was young. He had been busy working in the vegetable garden and came in to get a drink because he was thirsty. His master came in, saw him and said "don't take another drop of water until you dig a new well in the garden and drink from it".

This is an example of an evocative story. At the time, I thought that it meant "you think you've got it tough? You don't know the meaning of the word." Because the story created a very good narrative, and because it fits into the Zen story trope that is so well established, it stuck in my memory. Years later, I remembered it and I finally realized that the story isn't about water, but rather about finding my own individual source of inspiration or wisdom. I cannot repeat another person's wisdom---I have to find my own.

So why don't Daoist teachers just say "you need to find your own source of wisdom instead of listening to anyone else"? Well, once in a while I have found them be just that punk and plain. But being so obvious about the need for autonomy can be dangerous. It's one thing to think for yourself, it's another to act blindly on pre-conceived notions---and it can be very difficult to tell the difference between the two. That's why it's good to make the student have to work a bit first. Moreover, telling someone to "find your own source of wisdom" is contradictory. The point isn't to tell someone to think for themselves but rather to have them start doing it on their own. Evocative literature doesn't just hand people a lollypop and head them on their way. It gives them a riddle that they have to solve before they take the training wheels off.

The Different Frames Used to Study Daoism

One of the problems I often see when looking at Daoism is the "frame" that people use to look at it. That is to say, people approach it from a specific viewpoint based on their particular interest or area of expertise. Unfortunately, these folks often have zero appreciation of people who come to the subject from a different point of view. The result is often like the parable of the blind men and the elephant: everyone touches a very different part and comes up with very different ideas about the beast.

For example, people with personal experience with an individual sect sometimes make very definitive statements about Daoism in general. This is because they don't know anything about other sects (and there are a great many), or, the consensus amongst the scholarly community about its history and literature.

Also, some academics who focus on the culture of Daoism believe that only someone who is fluent in Chinese and who has spent a long time assimilating into traditional Chinese culture can have any affinity to Daoism. Moreover, they believe that long study in Daoist Temples under Chinese Daoist masters is essential. Anyone who studies books in translation and follows specific disciplines is merely fooling themselves if they believe that they are really "Daoists". The problem with this point of view is that it would seem to suggest that there is no objective "trans-cultural" core of Daoist philosophy or value in things like Daoist meditation techniques. It has mere aesthetic interest, but no more ultimate value than an ethnic cuisine or style of dress.

Other folks seem to see Daoism as primarily a mechanism for personal expression. One example of this are the folks who take it upon themselves to write "versions" of the Dao De Jing without educating themselves about the meaning of the original text. Another example are the guys who teach taijiquan as a "artistic dance" without trying to understand it as a martial art and holistic exercise system.

I don't really have much of a problem with any of these approaches as long as they aren't assumed to be the only one that has any legitimacy. Unfortunately, too many folks tend to assume that whoever isn't with them is---by definition---against them. I can see some merit in each of those frames. But in my own case I am approaching Daoism through the frame of practical philosophy. That is to say, I am looking through the entire tradition for ideas that have merit and how I can apply them to my everyday life.

Recommended Daoist Texts

There are a lot of Daoist books, there are a lot of English translations of these books, and, there are a lot of academic books about Daoism. Unfortunately, IMHO, most of them are not terribly helpful for someone who wants to use Daoism in their life. As I see it, the problem comes down the fact that very few authors really have the necessary qualifications.

First of all, most translators are experts at one thing, and one thing only: translations. And, unfortunately, even most native Chinese speakers don't really have a clue about Daoism. So why would someone who has never made the effort to study Daoism be able to understand what they are translating well enough to make it comprehensible to readers and not lose a lot of the nuances?

Other books are written by sociologists and historians who study Chinese society. They often are also skilled translators. But they are rarely actual practitioners of Daoism or philosophers. This limits their ability to understand what they are studying and their ability to communicate what knowledge they may have with others who are interested in integrating Daoism into their personal life. Moreover, as academics their job is to tease out differences between ancient

Chinese ways of looking at the world and modern ones, not identify similarities. This is useful for academic research, but can make books about Daoism almost impossible to understand by the general public. Moreover, university culture rewards writing that is boring, jargon-laden, and, obscure. This also makes many academic books extremely hard to understand by the general public.

Some academics see this as "a feature, not a bug" because they simply do not believe it is possible for non-Chinese, non-members of a Daoist religious sect to understand Daoism. Probably the most rabid exemplar of this position is Russell Kirkland. In his presentation "The Taoism of the Western Imagination and the Taoism of China: De-colonializing the Exotic Teachings of the East", he makes some very strong statements about not only the quality of many "translations", but also questions if it is even possible for anyone in the West to be a Daoist.

> *Perhaps an American today can indeed become "a Taoist." But if so, how and where can that really happen? Not, certainly, in an American bookstore, library, or classroom. I would say that if one travelled, for instance, to the Abbey of the White Clouds in Beijing, and underwent the spiritual training necessary to practice Taoism in the living tradition of "Complete Perfection," then a person of our society might be justified in claiming to "follow the Tao."*

....

> *If Taoism has something to offer the modern world, it is not to be found in the profitable inanities found on the shelves of American bookstores. Taoism is a religion of China, and it is studied by learning classical Chinese, by reading the great works of Taoism (which remain unknown to all but a handful of scholarly specialists), and by learning how to practice Taoism from real Taoists — from the living men and women of China who have maintained the ideals of Taoist tradition, and might be persuaded*

Russell Kirkland, Presented at the University of Tennessee, 20
October 1997. Available at the author's personal website.

I agree with Kirkland that there are a lot of terrible books about
Daoism. But I think he takes his position far too far. He believes that
there is no such thing as "philosophical" Daoism. His argument for
this point of view is based on his belief that there never were any
people in China who called themselves "Daoists" who would have
said this distinction (ie: between "philosophical" and "religious"
Daoism) exists. The problem with this argument is that while it might
be demonstrably true, it is irrelevant. The categories of
"philosophical" versus "religious" can be understood in sociological
terms, which is what Kirkland is doing. This involves looking at the
official theology, rituals, ecclesiastic organizations, historical
progression of ideas, etc. In contrast, if you look at Daoism using
philosophical terms---which is what I am trying to do in this book---
you only care about the ideas, not the culture. So, for example, it
doesn't matter from a philosophical analysis whether or not Zhuangzi
is a minor figure in institutional religious Daoism (one of Kirkland's
points) because all I care about is whether or not his ideas will help a
modern person live a better life. Indeed, you can look at almost any
text and try to understand the implicit philosophical ideas in it. This is
why, for example, there has been a proliferation of books like **Star
Wars and Philosophy**[3] and **Buffy the Vampire Slayer and
Philosophy: Fear and Trembling in Sunnydale**[4].

....

Some books are written by Daoist practitioners. But many of
them don't know English well enough to be able to be able to make
their ideas comprehensible. Others have pretty good English skills,
but don't have a wide enough education to be able to integrate Daoism
into the world of Western ideas. This dramatically limits their ability
to express complex, subtle concepts. Still others have gained their
knowledge about Daoism from only one specific source, and have no

---

3 Jason T. Eberl, Open Court, (March 23 2005), ISBN: 978-0812695830

4 James B. South and William Irwin (Editors) Open Court (March 21 2003), ISBN-10:
0812695313

knowledge at all about the broad range of different schools and sects in the Daoist universe. Many writers suffer from two or more of these problems.

Finally, very, very few people in general have an ability to express themselves in clear and precise language. Even worse, you can be an excellent writer and either not know much, or, be consciously writing garbage because you need the money and that's the only way you can get paid. Getting something published has very little to do with being a deep thinker and excellent writer. People get their stuff into print because they are very famous people and that will help sell books. Or, they support very popular "faddish" things that publishers think will sell books (hence the philosophy of Star Wars and Buffy books.) Or, they are part of an academic institution that ensures that anything they publish will be subsidized by various direct and indirect methods. Both academic and trade publishing are businesses, and no matter how brilliant and insightful a book might be, unless there is a way of making money off it, it simply will not get into print. As a result, a lot of terrible books get published. Conversely, I suspect that some insightful and profound manuscripts languish in the drawers of writers.

....

After a life time of reading, and, buying thousands of dollars worth of books the following are suggestions about what I think the basic library of Daoism should include for someone who is just starting out.

The Tao Te Ching, translated by Ellen M. Chen, First Edition 1989, "New Era Books", ISBN 1-55778-238-5 (pbk.)

Chen is an Chinese-born and trained scholar who taught at American universities. Her education immersed her in both Eastern and Western scholarly traditions, which means that she is able to at the same time understand the Laozi the way a Chinese person might, and also communicate it clearly to an educated native English speaker. What is even more important is that her translation comes with a commentary that explains the text according to her own personal Daoist worldview, which is religious. Chen sees Daoism as a religious movement aimed at integrating humanity into nature, which is identified as the Dao. As such she sees it as an outgrowth of the Shamanistic traditions of ancient pre-Chinese civilization. Moreover, she believes the appeal of Daoism for a modern audience is based on the pressing need to develop a modern worldview that will create a sustainable civilization. Having said the above, her commentary isn't preachy so much as insightful. She helps readers see some of the subtle complexity that is implied in the original text.

Wandering on the Way: Early Taoist Tales and Parables of Chuang Tzu, translated by Victor H. Mair, First Edition 1994, "Bantam Books", ISBN 0-553-37406-0.

Mair is a well-respected scholar, which is important. But one of the things I really like about this translation is the way he has made both the "loopiness", and, the innate common sense of the Zhuangzi available to the ordinary reader. For example, look at these two translations of the first paragraph of the chapter titled "Kengsang Ch'u"---the first by Herbert A. Giles and the second by Mair.

Among the disciples of Lao Tzŭ was one named Kên Sang Ch'u. He alone had attained to the Tao of his Master. He lived up north, on the Wei-lei Mountains. Of his attendants, he dismissed those who were systematically clever or conventionally charitable. The useless remained with him; the incompetent served him. And in three years the district of Wei-lei was greatly benefited.

Among the servants of Old Longears, there was a Kengsang Ch'u who had gotten a partial understanding of the Way of Old Longears. With it, he went north to dwell in the Jagged Mountains. He dismissed his attendants who were ostentatiously knowledgeable and distanced himself from his concubines were were insistently humane. He dwelled with rustics and made busy bees his servants. After he had dwelled there for three years, there was a great harvest at Jagged. ---[Mair doesn't end his translated paragraph in the same place as Giles.]

Zhuangzi is supposed to be strange and startling to read. But in a lot of translations this doesn't come through. A simple thing like trying to translate the proper names into English makes a huge difference, as they are often meant to be bizarre and referential to the issue at hand. Mair's translation also gives readers a lot more information than Giles. For example compare "systematically clever" versus "ostentatiously knowledgeable"---what is wrong with being "systematically clever"? But we do know that "ostentatiously knowledgeable" means "pompous windbag".

Also compare "The useless remained with him; the incompetent served him." with "He dwelled with rustics and made busy bees his servants." Obviously, Giles and Mair are both trying to translate something that is obscure in the original old Chinese, but Mair's version makes a sort of sense that Giles' doesn't. This is an important thing to remember. When you are translating an obscure, bizarre text---which the **Zhuangzi** is---the translator can easily fall into the trap of simply accepting anything that doesn't make immediate sense as being just "part of the paradox". But are "rustics" "useless people"? And if pollinators are the limiting factor on your farm, wouldn't hiring country folk to manage bee hives help increase the harvest? Even if this isn't literally what the original ancient Chinese meant, Mair's decision to translate it this way makes for an excellent evocative metaphor for someone who sees something that the non-realized man would miss.

Follow Giles' example and translate obscure passages as "mystical mumbo jumbo", and you end up with a book that reads like a fortune cookie. Mair, on the other hand, tries to make the seemingly strange and bizarre something that will make sense if you put effort into trying to understand it. As non-academics, none of us can actually read the original text and understand it. This means that we have to work with the translation in front of us. And I find that Mair's version of Zhuangzi is a valuable window into a very deep and profound way of looking at the world. Since I know that Mair is a respected academic and translator, I also know that there is at least a good argument for the way he has translated the text. If it is that hard to translate, I'll opt for the one that makes some sense to me rather than one that sounds like New Age snake oil.

Original Tao: Inward Training (Nei-Yeh) and the Foundations of Taoist Mysticism, translated by Harold D. Roth, first edition 1999, Columbia University Press, ISBN 978-0-231-11564-3

This is a book that the vast majority of people interested in Daoism have probably never heard about. That's too bad, because it comes from the same source and time as the much more popular Laozi. Oddly enough, it has never actually been "lost" and rediscovered so much as it managed to "hide in plain sight" from Western scholars. The book was preserved as a chapter of the Guanzi. This is a large text that deals primarily with philosophical issues relating to state governance from distinctly non-Daoist points of view. People who wanted to read the Guanzi weren't interested in Daoist meditation techniques, and people interested in Daoist meditation would not have wanted to read the Guanzi. As a result, the book was invisible to scholars.

The fascinating thing is that it dates back to the same time as the ***Laozi*** and appears to have come from the same cultural source. People naively assume that each of the key texts of Daoism was written by a single individual: Laozi, Zhuangzi, and, Liezi. But the fact of the matter is that all of them grew out of a conversation or dialectic within a segment of ancient Chinese society. In some cases, there seems to have been an oral tradition that then migrated to written. In all cases there were additions and subtractions as the texts went through different editions. In effect, there was a long process of "natural selection" that resulted in the texts we have today. So looking at the ***Nei-Yeh*** allows people to understand the context that the ***Laozi*** emerged from. And, that context was one in which people actually followed specific meditation practices.

> *Those who can transform even a single thing, call the "numinous";*
>
> *Those who can alter even a single situation, call them "wise".*
>
> *But to transform without expending vital energy; to alter without expending wisdom:*

Only exemplary persons who hold fast to the One
are able to do this.

Hold fast to the One; do not lose it,

And you will be able to master the myriad things.

Exemplary persons act upon things,

And are not acted upon by them,

Because they grasp the guiding principle of the
One.

(**Nei-yeh**, Chapter IX, Harold D. Roth translator)

"Holding onto the One" is the idea that one people should try to remember in each moment that the Dao pervades and permeates all of the world and everything we do. It is easy to forget the way things interact and the subtle relationships and laws that govern those interactions. We get "lost in the moment" and forget that we are living human beings that can choose to "buy into" or "disengage" with every opportunity we are presented with---even if it means simply reminding yourself that you have a choice to get angry or not about some unavoidable indignity that the world is imposing upon you. And when we forget about "the One" we forget the subtle yet profound influences that we can exert without exerting ourselves. The wise woman realizes that the right word or the little push in the right place can create a huge effect as it cascades through our environment---but she can only do this if she holds fast to the idea that this is possible if she is sensitive to the subtle world around her. This is "holding onto the One".

This is where Kirkland's annoyance with the idea of "philosophical Daoism" comes from. If you look at the other key Daoist texts---**Laozi, Zhuangzi**, and, **Liezi**---you will see that spiritual practices are an essential element of the tradition. This is not the same thing as saying that all real Daoism is religious, however. It is possible to believe in mental discipline through regular practice without submitting the control of an ecclesiastic hierarchy, and/or, blindly follow fundamentally obscure texts and traditions. But it is true that a lot of people in the West who call themselves "Daoists" totally reject the idea that to be a Daoist involves some sort of personal, regular spiritual program. The ***Nei-yeh*** is useful because it shows that spiritual practice is not some sort of "add on" that those awful religious Daoists stuck onto pristine "philosophical Daoism", but rather something that was integral to the idea from the get-go.

The Book of Lieh-tzŭ: A Classic of Tao, translated by A. C. Graham, first edition 1960, Columbia University Press, ISBN 0-231-07236-8.

This is another book that most Westerners would not have heard of. I recall reading, however, that this is the classic book on Daoism that Chinese speakers would most likely know. That's worth something in itself. It is very much in the same mold as the ***Zhuangzi***, indeed they both share some of the same stories. But it adds others that are equally biting in the way they attack conventional wisdom and suggest that people should pay more attention to the way things really are.

I'm suggesting the A. C. Graham version because as an academic translation it attempts to stay close to the original meaning of the book. To understand this point, compare these two versions. The first is from the most popular "translation", the Shambhala book ***Lieh-tzu: A Taoist Guide to Practical Living*** by Eva Wong. (Oddly enough, Eva Wong is a fellow initiate into the same Temple as I---although we have never met.)

> *Lieh-tzu left his home in Cheng and journeyed to the kingdom of Wei. While walking down a dusty road, he saw the remains of a skull lying by the wayside. Lieh-tzu saw that it was the skull of a human that was over a hundred years old. He picked up the bone, brushed the dirt off it, and looked at it for a while. Finally, he put the skull down, sighed, and said to his student who was standing nearby. "In this world only you and I understand life and death." Turning to the skull he*

said, "Are you unfortunate to be dead and we fortunate to be alive? Maybe it is you who are fortunate and we who are unfortunate!"

Lieh-tzu then said to his student , "Many people sweat and toil, and feel satisfied that they have accomplished many things. However, in the end we are not all that much different from this polished piece of bone. In a hundred years, everyone we know will be just a pile of bones. What is there to gain in life, and what is there to lose in death?"

The ancients knew that life cannot go on forever, and death is not the end of everything. Therefore, they are not excited by the event of life nor depressed by the occurrence of death. Birth and death are part of the natural cycle of things. Only those who can see through the illusions of life and death can be renewed with heaven and earth and age with the sun, moon and stars.

Liezi, "translated" by Eva Wong, from the first chapter

Now let's look at Graham's version.

When Lieh-tzŭ was eating at the roadside on a journey to Wei, he saw a skull a hundred years old. He picked a stalk, pointed at it, and said, turning to his disciple Pai-feng:

"Only he and I know that you were never born and will never die. Is it he who is truly miserable, is it we who are truly happy?

"Within the seeds of things there are germs. When they find water they develop in successive stages. Reaching water on the edge of land, they become a scum. Breeding on the bank, they become the plantain. When the plantain reaches dung, it

*becomes the crowfoot. The root of the crowfoot
becomes woodlice, the leaves become butterflies.
The butterfly suddenly changes into an insect which
breeds under the stove and looks as though it has
shed its skin, named the ch'ü-to. After a thousand
days the ch'ü-to changes into a bird named the kan-
yü-ku. The saliva of the kan-yü-ku becomes the ssŭ-
mi, which becomes the vinegar animalcula yi-lu,
which begets the animalcula huang-k'uang, which
begets the chiu-yu, which begets the gnat, which
begets the firefly.*

*[etc, etc, more and more transformations, ending
in---]*

*The yang-hsi, combining with an old bamboo which
has not put forth shoots, begets the ch'ing-ning.
This begets the leopard, which begets the horse,
which begets man. Man in due course returns to the
germs. All the myriad things come out of germs and
go back to germs.*

Liezi, "Heaven's Gifts", A. C. Graham translator

Compare these two passages. It's obvious that Wong is trying to
simplify the text to make it more appealing to the general reader. But
she takes huge liberties with it. For example, in her version Liezi
picks up the skull and makes a comment saying that only Liezi and
the student know about life and death. In Graham's version, Liezi says
only he and the skull know. This is an enormous difference!

Things get worse after that. Wong dispenses with the original's
long blah-blah-blah about transformations. But by doing so, it totally
changes the meaning of the text. In Wong's version Liezi makes the
vague statement that "death is not the end of everything"---which
could mean that he supports some sort of immortality, or, that he is
simply saying that just because you die doesn't mean that everyone
else does too. She ends with another vague bromide: "Only those
who can see through the illusions of life and death can be renewed

with heaven and earth and age with the sun, moon and stars." What exactly does this mean?

In Graham's version Liezi goes on about "transformation" (which is a tremendously important Daoist concept.) It is hard to understand exactly what he is talking about, because his knowledge of biology is so tremendously primitive compared to our own. Is he implying some sort of evolutionary theory? Or is he suggesting some sort of atomic theory whereby matter gets absorbed into the bodies of other creatures through the process of growth and decay? It is very clear, however, that what he is talking about is material and scientific in nature, not some sort of spiritual or metaphysical process of life after death.

Wong is an example of someone who practices Daoism and is a native Chinese speaker but who doesn't have the scholarly education to understand the ancient Chinese text and the complex constellation of ideas that it emerged from. As a result, she can't "tease out" the important subtleties that Graham does. The result is a "fortune cookie" translation that sounds profound, but really doesn't give the reader anything useful.

Another point. The four books I've mentioned so far are all obviously linked together in some way or another. We know this because they share sections. The passage from the **Liezi** is almost exactly the same in Mair's translation of **Zhuangzi**. You wouldn't know this if you had only read Wong's version. This is an important thing to learn. Daoism was an actual movement in ancient China and modern Western readers need to remember this. A lot of people are content to just read and re-read the **Laozi** over and over again without even attempting to study anything else. This is silly. There are other texts out there that people can learn from, so why not?

One last point about the **Liezi**. Graham's translation can be a bit of a hard slog for the general reader. It varies widely in readability and the translator intrudes a lot to explain things. Unfortunately, this is because the original text really is widely variable in quality. But the effort is worth it, because some of the passages are really interesting. For example:

> *There was a man who lost his axe, and suspected*
> *the boy next door. He watched the boy walking: he*

*had stolen the axe! His expression, his talk, his
behaviour, his manner, everything about him
betrayed that he had stolen the axe.*

*Soon afterwards the man was digging in his garden
and found the axe. On another day he saw the boy
next door again; nothing in his behaviour and
manner suggested that he would steal an axe.*

Liezi, "Explaining Conjunctions", A. C. Graham translator

Process Versus Substance

There is something about Western society that encourages people
to look at the world as being composed of "things". In significant
ways, Daoism is different---it teaches us to look at the world as
"process".

What is a river? We give them names, draw them on maps---but
they are really just a prediction that a large number of water droplets
will be moving down hill in a particular place. The ancient Greek
philosopher Heraclitus pointed out this fact in his quote that "No man
ever steps in the same river twice". The point he was making is that
even though we talk as if what we call a "river" is a thing, actually, it
is a process, namely, the process of a myriad of water droplets moving
down hill.

What we call a "river" is actually one part of a "homeostatic
process" known as the water cycle. That is the system where water
gets evaporated, falls as precipitation on high ground, then flows
downstream, where it evaporates, moves as vapour over high ground,
then falls as precipitation again, to flow downstream all over again. A
homeostatic process is one where a certain degree of stability is
maintained through positive and negative feedback. In the case of the
water cycle, naturally occurring mechanisms such as swamps, beaver
dams, and, glaciers regulate the flow of water to ensure that a river
has a constant flow instead of simply drying up when there is no rain.

Another example of homeostasis is the flame of a candle. The
heat melts wax, which allows it to flow through the wick and feed the
flame. This in turn melts more wax, which continues the practise. This

allows for a more-or-less consistent flame from when the candle is first lit until it completely burns up.

What is important about this idea of homeostasis is the implication for how humanity views itself. The Western world rejected Heraclitus' ideas and instead embraced those of Plato, who believed in the idea that all of the world consists of 'things'. Even ideas existed as objects, which he called the 'Forms'. Ultimately this notion resulted in the idea that what makes people "people" is a specific thing, which is called a soul. Most people are aware of the first half of Heraclitus' saying, but not the second: "No man ever steps in the same river twice, for it's not the same river and he's not the same man." I suspect that Heraclitus would not suggest that human beings have souls.

....

I believe that many Daoists would agree with Heraclitus. They do not look at the world as a collection of things, but rather of processes, which they call "daos". And embracing all of the minor daos, is one great process, known as the "Dao". People sometimes equate the Dao to God. But that misses the point. The God of the West is a being (which is just a type of thing), whereas the Dao is simply a homeostatic process that governs all of the universe. Daoists do not seek the mind of God to explain why something happens. Instead, they look for the general process that has manifested in a specific example.

Transformations and Kungfu

Chinese folk culture believes that creatures can transform themselves from one thing to another. The famous Chinese novel Journey to the West is filled with these beings. Indeed, the very first part of the most popular version of this book, **A Taoist Interpretation of Journey to the West,** begins with this poem:

> *Before Chaos was divided, Heaven and Earth were one;*
>
> *All was a shapeless blur, and no men had appeared.*

Journey to the West, W. J. F. Jenner translator, Foreign Languages Press, 1993, (ISBN: 978-7-119-01663-4)

In this book the lead character, Monkey, is born of a stone. One of the "villains" is a gold fish from the goddess Guan Yin's pond that becomes a mighty dragon. Laozi's ox becomes another monster. Monkey's right-hand-whatever is Pigsy, who was a heavenly general that was reincarnated as a man-pig hybrid monster that was converted into a protector through the intervention of the Bodhisattva Guanyin. Even less fanciful books take the idea of transformation for granted. In The Three Kingdoms when Cao Cao decides to build a new palace he needs a large beam for it. The only tree large enough is an immense and ancient pear tree. When woodsmen set to chop it down, it bleeds from their axe cuts and screams in agony! Even a very realistic novel like The Dream of the Red Chamber starts with the premise that a stone transforms itself into sentience and sets out to be incarnated as a human being to see what that type of life is like.

These are literary devices, of course, but they are very different from the sort of thing one finds in European literature. I cannot think of any example in English, French, German, Russian, etc, literature where animals or plants work themselves into some semblance of humanity. The most one can think of are things like witches' "familiar spirits"---which are totally different because they are actually demons masquerading as animals, not animals becoming humans.

....

What is at work here is a key Daoist concept: kung fu. Everyone has heard of this term through Bruce Lee and Jackie Chan movies. But while martial arts are examples of kung fu, just about any activity can be a kung fu. That's because kung fu just means "excellence through diligent training". Kung fu can be done through just about any activity---you can achieve kung fu in art, the skilled trades, or even something as lowly as being a janitor. The important issue isn't what you are doing, but rather what attitude you bring to it.

Someone who practices kung fu isn't focused on results but rather the process. And "process" is meant in a different way from how most people would understand the term. For someone practicing kung fu, there is a constant self-evaluation going on. This includes things like awareness of the posture, muscle tension, how one breathes and so on. It also involves thinking about the mental state. Are you distracted? Thinking about the fight you had with your spouse last night? It also involves thinking about the "big picture". Why exactly am I doing this task anyway? People who don't understand the ideal of kung fu will admit that people who pursue it can often achieve amazing results. But that isn't the point. Kung fu is a spiritual discipline aimed at squeezing every last iota of self-awareness from the experience of being alive. In the process of doing so, one gains a deeper insight into the subtle processes that govern how our minds and body work, how the universe we inhabit operates, and, how we interact with it.

The process of doing one kung fu---for example the martial arts---will inevitably bleed into the rest of your life. If you spend a lot of time really thinking deeply about how your body and mind operates while training in a studio, you will inevitably carry the same attitude into the rest of your life. What this means is that kung fu inevitably becomes the practice of holding onto the One: the process of reminding yourself to look for the subtle individual daos, and, the single over-arching Dao, that govern our experiences as human beings. Carry this discipline throughout your life and eventually you will become something of a "realized man". That is the ideal of Daoism, the person who has---through careful observation of both self and the world around her---realized the basic principles that govern everything and in the process transformed themselves into something quite remarkable.

Male Versus Female

People associate Daoism with the Yin Yang symbol. The idea is that there are two elements in life that balance each other. One way of applying this dualism is to see the world as being divided into male and female. Balance comes from accepting both equally. Even though Daoism accepts the necessity of both elements embodied in the Yin Yang, it suggests that we should have a preference for the feminine over the masculine. In contrast, Western society is profoundly sexist and anti-feminine. It has been this way for so for so long and so deeply that it can be very hard to recognize this as bias. Instead, it just seems "obviously true".

....

Men are supposedly more courageous than women. They are also more "stoic" and able to suffer pain. That's why only men have traditionally been soldiers. But if that is the case, consider this old European saying: "Women fight their battles on the birthing chair". Even today giving birth is tremendously painful and still sometimes dangerous. Before modern medicine---and especially during the early industrial revolution---it was often fatal. Health issues aside, being a single mother is often a sentence to a lifetime of brutal poverty. Yet how often has anyone heard a woman say that they are too afraid to have a child? Men who fight in battles have to conquer their fears, but so do women when they get pregnant.

....

Since 9/11 fire fighting has become our definition of a heroic job. Firemen run into burning buildings to save lives, which is something most of us would hesitate to do. But I'd like to offer another example that should be put alongside these men: nurses. If SARS, Ebola, or, Marburg virus hits you, there is probably going to be a woman wearing protective gear who is going to take your blood, and, wipe up your vomit and diarrhea, and maybe even hold your hand. She knows that no matter what precautions she takes, she might still get sick, and maybe even die. Yet, she still does it. Nurses are just as much heroes as firefighters! They can be soft, wear perfume, etc, but they sometimes have to be really brave to do their jobs.

....

Men are big and strong. They work in construction and use big heavy tools, carry bags of concrete, throw around cement blocks and so on. Women just aren't strong enough to do that sort of thing. Well, elephants can carry weights that would crush a man. In the grand scheme of things, the average man is only slightly stronger than the average woman. A strong man can pick up an eighty-pound bag of concrete to load a cement mixer---but he can't pick up a one hundred and eighty-pound bag. So what if the average strong woman can only pick up a forty-pound bag? She will just have to move two bags instead of one. The problem isn't that women are inherently the "weaker sex", it's rather that the tools and materials of jobs like construction are designed around a specific, masculine idea of what a person can or cannot lift. Change the design criteria, and most women could work in male-dominated fields, like the trades.

....

There is nothing at all wrong with being a man. But we live in a profoundly sexist culture. And in the process of putting women down, we have also created a stereotypical description of what it means to be a human being. We do this by putting down those particular attributes that we associate with femininity. Women are supposed to be subtle, nurturing, concerned about feelings, and, supportive. Men are supposed to be dynamic, creative, analytical, and, competitive. There is nothing inherently wrong with any of these ideals. But if any of them become over-emphasized, they can damage individuals and society.

If we favour action to the point of discouraging attention to subtleties we start doing things by brute force which is both destructive and wasteful. If we favour creating the new to the point of becoming indifferent to what we already have, we will eliminate many important and useful things---often before we even understand their value. If we reduce every decision to a simple rationalist calculus and ignore the concerns of people who cannot express themselves in that framework, we run the risk of making catastrophic mistakes simply because we refused to see the problem from a different perspective. And, if we reduce all human interaction to a competition, we will lose the opportunity to gain the advantages that accrue from co-operation.

Daoists emphasize feminine qualities because in a profoundly sexist society it is the only way to reassert balance.

Hard Versus Soft, or, Keeping Your Spirit "Whole"

At one point in my taijiquan training I was taught how to take a punch. What I had to do was stand in a particular stance and another student hit me as hard as he could on the chest. If I flinched or tightened up the result was a horrible bruise that would last for weeks. But I learned that if I kept totally relaxed the force of the punch would flow through my rib cage, into my spine, and through my legs and feet into the floor. This isn't a metaphor. I could feel the force flow like an electric current through my body---leaving me totally unharmed.

The soft overcame the hard.

This wasn't the result of some occult power. It was just that the inherent resilience of my bodily structure is enough to avoid injury as long as I don't "freeze" it by tensing my muscles. It's exactly the same principle that a high school chemistry teacher shows when he dips a rubber ball in liquid nitrogen and the shatters it like glass when he tries to bounce it off the floor.

....

Zhuangzi relates that Confucius was once watching a huge cataract: "No tortoise, alligator, fish or turtle could swim there." Yet he was surprised to see an old man swimming in the middle of the rapids. Thinking that he had fallen in, Confucius sent his disciples out along the river to try to save him. After a while, this fellow came out of the water on his own, which amazed the sage.

> *Confucius followed after the man and inquired of*
> *him, saying, "I thought you were a ghost, but when*
> *I looked more closely I saw that you are a man.*

(Zhuangzi, "Outer Chapters", "Understanding Life", Section
Eight, Victor Mair trans.)

Instead of fighting against the current, the old man flowed with it.
When the current pushed him away from his destination, he let
himself go with it. When it pushed him towards it, he added a few
strokes. Before long, he arrived where he wanted to go.

Being soft is not the same thing as being weak. Instead, it about
being "non-resisting".

....

And non-resisting is not about just deciding to be non-resistant.
Tensing up before the fist hits you is not a voluntary response---it is
instinctive. So being "soft" requires more than just a conscious
decision, it requires a revolution in your being. Zhuangzi talks about
this at length. He has Liezi (a master of the Dao) ask another sage
(Director Yin) about what is required.

"The ultimate man can walk under water without drowning, can tread upon fire without feeling hot, and can soar above the myriad things without fear. May I ask how he achieves this?"

"It's because he guards the purity of his vital breath," said Director Yin, *"it's not a demonstration of his expertise or daring.*

He goes on to give a revealing example.

"If a drunk falls from a carriage, even if it is going very fast, he will not die. His bones and joints are the same as those of other people, but the injuries he receives are different. It's because his spirit is whole. He was not aware of getting into the carriage, nor was he aware of falling out of it. Life and death, alarm and fear do not enter his breast. Therefore, he confronts things without apprehension. If someone who has gotten his wholeness from wine is like this, how much more so would one be who gets his wholeness from heaven! The sage hides within his heavenly qualities, thus nothing can harm him..."

(Zhuangzi, "Understanding Life", Part Two, Mair trans)

....

Yet another example comes from a boatman.

Yen Yǔan inquired of Confucius, saying, "When I was crossing the gulf of Goblet Deep, the ferryman handled the boat like a spirit. I asked him about it, saying, 'Can handling a boat be learned?' 'Yes', said he, 'good swimmers can learn quickly. As for divers, they can handle a boat right away without ever having seen one.' I asked him why this was so, but he didn't tell me. I venture to ask what you think he meant."

*"A good swimmer can learn quickly because he
forgets about the water," said Confucius. "As for a
diver being able to handle a boat right away
without ever having seen one, it's because he
regards the watery depths as if they were a mound
and the capsizing of a boat as if it were the rolling
back of a carriage. Capsizing and rolling back
could unfold a myriad times before him without
affecting his heart, so he is relaxed wherever he
goes."*

Confucius then goes on and gives another example that stresses
the importance of keeping your "spirit whole"

*"He who competes for a piece of tile displays all of
his skill; he competes for a belt buckle gets
nervous; he who competes for gold gets flustered.
His skill is still the same, but there is something that
distracts him and causes him to focus on externals.
Whoever focuses on externals will be clumsy
inside."*

(Zhuangzi, "Understanding Life", Part Three, Mair trans)

The archer who is competing for a prize is not afraid of drowning
or getting nasty bruises. But his mind is distracted from the act of
shooting his bow by considering what he would do with his prize.
This is the point of the following apocryphal story:

*A martial arts student went to his teacher and said
earnestly, "I am devoted to studying your martial
system. How long will it take me to master it."*

*The teacher's reply was casual, "Ten years."
Impatiently, the student answered, "But I want to
master it faster than that. I will work very hard. I
will practice everyday, ten or more hours a day if I
have to. How long will it take then?"*

38

....

Being "soft" instead of "hard" is a relatively easy concept to understand. But how one becomes truly "soft" is not. "Hardness" involves separating yourself from the universe (or Dao) around you. That punching exercise that I introduced this section was not called "taking a punch" in my school, but rather "exchanging energy". It was not considered a skill that was to be developed to protect you in a fight, but a way of helping one another to develop a deeper understanding of the Dao.

Sitting and Forgetting, or, Mind Fasting

One of the things I learned when I was at a Daoist retreat centre was a form of meditation called "just sitting". And that's all they taught. You sat on a cushion and all the teacher did was walk around correcting your posture if you were slouching. You weren't expected to sit in a lotus posture or anything, you just sat as comfortably as possible. Nor were you supposed to sit for any specified length of time. If you found it too difficult to sit any longer, you were supposed to stop.

What was that all about?

....

Sir Motley of Southurb sat leaning against his low table. He looked up to heaven and exhaled slowly. Disembodied, he seemed bereft of soul. Sir Wanderer of Countenance Complete, who stood in attendance before him, asked, "How can we explain this? Can the body really be made to become like withered wood? Can the mind really be made to become like dead ashes? The one who is leaning against the table now is not the one who was formerly leaning against the table."

Zhuangzi, "On the Equality of Things", Mair trans.

"I'm making progress," said Yen Hui.

"What do you mean?" asked Confucius.

"I have forgotten rites and music."

"Not bad, but you still haven't got it."

Yen Hui saw Confucius again on another day and said, "I'm making progress."

"What do you mean?"

"I have forgotten humaneness and righteousness."

"Not bad, but you still haven't got it."

Yen Hui saw Confucius again on another day and said, "I'm making progress."

"What do you mean?"

"I sit and forget."

"What do you mean, 'sit and forget'?" Confucius asked with surprise.

"I slough off my limbs and trunk," said Yen Hui, "dim my intelligence, depart from my form, leave knowledge behind, and become identical with the Transformational Thoroughfare. This is what I mean by 'sit and forget'."

"If you are identical," said Confucius, "then you have no preferences. If you are transformed, then

Zhuangzi, "The Great Ancestral Teacher", Mair trans.

What these two posts are talking about is Zuowang, or "sitting
and forgetting". A respected scholar of Daoism, Livia Kohn, describes
this as: "a state of deep trance or intense absorption, during which no
trace of ego-identity is felt and only the underlying cosmic current of
the Dao is perceived as real" (from the Wikipedia.) Zhuangzi is
describing the ultimate goal of "just sitting", which is "sitting and
forgetting". What is it that people are supposed to be forgetting? I'd
suggest that they are the delusions that cloud our minds and cut us off
from the world as it really is.

....

The thing about formal meditation practices is that no matter
what you do, you are really only doing one particular thing, and, when
you do it, you are prey to one particular problem. The thing you are
doing is learning about your thinking. And the problem you face is
that the act of thinking about thinking gets in the way of observing
and learning about thinking.

When you are sitting on the mats meditating, you will notice that
there are a lot of thoughts that rattle through your mind. "My legs
hurt." "What will I have for supper?" "Is my wife OK?"---and so on.
If you stick with the practice over a long period of time, people
generally start to find that their minds quiet down. Usually this
involves some practice like taking deep breaths and counting them.
"One, two, three, four, five,"---and so on. You will notice that you get
distracted "That jerk at work so annoyed me today! Oh, yeah. I'm
supposed to be meditating. One, two, three, four, five. Damn the boss!
He shouldn't allow that jerk to get away with---. Oh yeah, meditation.
One, two, three, four, Who does he think he is anyway! One, two,
three, four---". Oh crap. I forgot to meditate. I'm never going---.
Whoops! One, two, three, four, five---".

The thing about meditation is to observe this rattling, chattering,
distracting "monkey mind" that intrudes on your existence. If you
calm yourself and pay attention to it, the noise will begin to slowly

drift away. You will gradually find that you can sit and count up to ten or twenty for longer and longer periods without being distracted by your thoughts. Other distractions will begin to present themselves, however. You will probably start falling asleep. But if you stick to the practice, day after day, and this too will pass. Many people then start to hallucinate. In my case, for example, one time I was sitting in meditation and suddenly I found myself downhill skiing at very high velocity.

These phenomena are different from person to person, but predictable percentages of the population will manifest them in any given group. In fact, they are so predictable that the meditation master who taught me had a volunteer who's job it was to stand by with towels in case someone started to cry uncontrollably. I've seen this happen. A woman started to weep so much that she was given a towel to dry herself off. Later, I also went through a long period when I wept so much while meditating that each time I got off the cushion so many tears had flowed into my lap that I looked like I had peed my pants.

The great thing about this predictability is that it allows people to teach these methods with a fair degree of confidence that if someone sticks to the practice they will eventually gain the ability to quiet down and experience moments of clarity and peace with greater and greater regularity. And this new experience isn't just relegated to time spent on the cushions. In your day-to-day life you will also find that you are more peaceful, centred, and, have greater insight into how your own mind works. This will bleed over into having a better understanding about how other people's minds work, and, what subtle rules govern the world around you.

....

As I said earlier, however, there is also a universal problem with meditation.

Early on I suggested that meditation is about dispelling delusions. These come in many sizes and shapes. Of course, what I've called the "monkey mind" is the source of many of them. They can be things like "I'm no good", "I'm too fat", and so on. Others are subtle, such as "I simple cannot do that!" For example, I once saw a historical movie about King Charles the 2nd of England. His father had been deposed by revolutionaries and executed, and the son was living in exile with his mother. The scene showed her complaining bitterly because she had to eat off china plates that had been used before, washed and used again (ie: just like everyone else.) She felt that this was disgusting. Her son was appalled at this delusional thinking, but was forced to humour her in order to keep harmony in the family.

Outside of royal households delusions also reign supreme. People buy expensive homes that they cannot afford. People pursue careers that kill them with stress and over work. People piss away money that their families desperately need. People refuse to admit that people with different skin colour are human beings just like them. People complain bitterly about any attempt to build a sustainable society and deny the reality of climate change. A moment's thought will provide lots of examples. Sitting and forgetting is a wonderful corrective to delusional thinking because once you learn to quiet down the monkey mind, you gain the clarity to see your own personal delusions for what they are.

This is a general truth with, however, ONE ENORMOUS CAVEAT!!!!!!!!!! In the New Testament Jesus talks about people looking to remove a speck of dust from another person's eye while walking around with a huge wooden beam in their own. The human mind is a very subtle and inventive thing, when we drive away the delusions we can see, invisible ones will try to move in and replace them. Some of the delusions that come from meditation are:

1. an excessive love of peace and quiet, to the point of no longer being able to function around ordinary people
2. an unwillingness to engage in society, to the point of refusing to work together for political issues, doing charitable work, or, being a useful member of the community
3. a belief in the ultimate metaphysical importance of "spiritual things": for example, believing that simply meditating for long periods of time makes the world a better place all by itself
4. becoming obsessed with teaching what you have learned through meditation to other people, whether or

> not they are capable of, or even interested in, learning
> it

5. becoming addicted to altered states of consciousness
and losing the ability to function in the world of
ordinary people

Some of these delusions can grow into full-blown manias. A very small percentage of people will even develop real psychiatric problems and require treatment. Unfortunately, many people teaching meditation techniques tend to be people holding onto one of the subtle delusions (eg: that meditation is a universal panacea that will solve all problems) which keeps them from understanding how it can lead to its own delusions and be outright dangerous for some.

A Daoist teaching book expresses the danger of excessive meditation through a story about an initiate who finds himself living a life of contemplation in a cave. One day he meets someone who teaches him a lesson.

---Hao T'ai-ku walked out of his cave to enjoy the peace and quiet of the surroundings. He noticed a man sitting under one of the arches of the bridge. The man was polishing a stone. Occasionally he would take the polished stone and look at it for a while, then he would resume polishing. He would polish a single stone until it becames so thin that it disintegrated; then he would pick up another stone and begin the process all over again. Hao T'ai-ku thought this behaviour strange and decided to ask the man the purpose of his activity. He said, "Sir, it appears that you are polishing stones for nothing. Your activity does not seem to lead to any accomplishment. What are you trying to do? Maybe I can help." The man replied, "I am trying to make a mirror by polishing the stone." Hao T'ai-ku said, "People make mirrors by polishing bronze, not stones. If you keep on polishing stones, you will never get what you want." The man laughed and said, "You are telling me that if I stubbornly sit here and polish my stones, I shall never make a mirror!

*What about you? Do you think that by sitting here
stubbornly in the cave you can become an
immortal?" Hao T'tai-ku realized what the man
was trying to teach him by his actions. But as he
was about to ask this strange man for more
instructions, the man suddenly disappeared. Hao
T'ai-ku said to himself, "The sage was right.
Stubbornly sitting here all the time is 'dead
sitting.'" He went back into the cave, collected his
belongings, and left the area.*

Seven Taoist Masters: a Folk Novel of China, chapt 16 trans by
Eva Wong. Shambhala, first published 1990, (ISBN: O-87773-544-1)

Sitting and forgetting is a wonderful practice to help people live
better lives. But if it becomes an end in itself or reinforces a
delusional belief system, it becomes yet another way of estranging
yourself from the world around you.

Holding onto the One

Another type of meditation practice is known as shou-i, or,
"holding onto the One". Harold D. Roth describes this practice as

*---holding fast to the One entails retaining a sense
or a vision of the Way as the one unifying force
within phenomenal reality while seeing this reality
in all its complexity. "*

(Original Tao, Harold D. Roth trans and commentary, Chapter 3,
part XIII)

Whereas sitting and forgetting was about finding a quiet place to
sit and ignore the world around you so you can focus on how your
mind operates, holding onto the One is something that you try to do
every other moment of your waking life. It is about reminding
yourself to be aware of your surroundings and look for the subtle
forces at play in it. If you remind yourself to look for subtleties, you
will eventually begin to see them. And when you do, you will find
yourself being able to achieve interesting results.

Let me give an illustrative example. Where I work I was once approached by a student who wanted the Library to install public computer printers that were able to print on both sides of a sheet of paper---to help the environment. I'm too low on the food-chain to have any influence, but I explained to him a strategy for getting his suggestion implemented.

I told him that there would be no sense at all trying to make a suggestion to any individual manager, as it would be ignored. Primarily, this is because he would just consider this proposal extra work with no value to his career. The solution, therefore, would be to do all the work for the manager and to submit the proposal in a venue where it would be visible to the manager's boss. The way to do this, therefore, was for him to write up a detailed proposal outlining the costs involved plus a source for the new printing equipment. This meant the manager really didn't have to do any work. And instead of just sending this proposal to the person who managed the public printers, I suggested he send the suggestion to the Library "Question and Answer Board". Since all of these submissions went directly to the Associate Chief Librarian---who then passed them onto relevant managers with her comments attached---it would be impossible for the relevant manager to simply ignore, because it would be coming from his boss instead of just a student.

I outlined this strategy by first asking the student "Do you really want to get these printers changed?" That is because a lot of times people just want to vent, but can't be bothered to do any heavy lifting. The guy surprised me by saying "yes, I do". And he also surprised me by actually following my suggestion. Two weeks later, I saw his detailed proposal posted on the Q and A board, and by the end of the semester the printers had been upgraded to do double-sided printing.

Holding onto the One has obvious similarities to Buddhist "mindfulness". Both of them require reminding yourself that you exist and are an observer to your existence. Both are against "losing yourself in your delusions". But holding onto the One has the added emphasis on looking for the subtle "Daos" that exist in our environment. In the example I gave above, I was explaining to the student the Dao of bureaucracy and how he could use my knowledge to exert some kung fu on it.

....

Learning to hold onto the One is also a mental project, just like sitting and forgetting. You have to be aware of what your mind is doing to be able to really see what is happening in the world around you. You have to be calm to see what is in front of you. You also need to be aware of your biases if you are going to have some sort of objective viewpoint. So holding onto the One is also a process of learning about how your mind operates. And just as sitting and forgetting has potential dangers, so does holding onto the One.

If not done properly, the practice of constant careful observation can lead to an inability to ever relax and simply "be in the moment". That too is important. In Japanese Zen this ability to just act without thinking is known as "mushin no shin" or "mind without mind". It is an integral part of martial arts training, but it also blends into all of human life. To give an example, while sparring in taijiquan (ie: "push hands" or tuishou) sometimes I have had the experience of "just acting" totally without any forethought. The result is often that someone flies through the air, or, gets pinned with a joint lock. This is an interesting phenomenon, but paradoxically, to understand it you have to be willing to make the effort to hold onto the One and carefully observe the way your mind operates.

Consider the act of speaking or writing. Did you choose the particular word you just spoke? Perhaps you did, but how often do you stop and make the time to do that? In writing this book there have been times when I had to stop and think about exactly what word I wish to write. And, of course, I am constantly looking at the text and making changes to "polish it" to the point where it will be published. But even when I stop and make changes, the words just "pop" into existence. Again, think about the act of choosing. Did you choose the word you use? If so, did you "choose to choose" that word? Or did you just act? And even if you did "choose to choose", did you "choose to choose to choose"? The point I am trying to make is that even in the most carefully contrived and worked-over human decision, there is ultimately an experience of a thought or action just popping into existence.

Zhuangzi, "Autumn Floods", part 2, Mair translation

It is possible for someone trying to hold onto the One to forget this fact and change from observing the way things really are to fretting about how things should be, or, how things come about. This gets in the way of the spontaneous generation of new actions and thoughts. This situation is like the story of the centipede that was found paralyzed by the side of the road. When asked what happened, she answered by saying that someone asked her how she could control all her different legs. Once she started thinking about the question, she lost the ability to walk. She had succumbed to "analysis paralysis".

Don't let that happen to you!

Internal Alchemy, Taijiquan, and, Qigong

In addition to sitting and forgetting, and, holding onto the One, there is another important Daoist meditation system. It's called "qigong" ("chi kung" using Wade/Giles.) Actually, the term originally used was "neidan", or "internal alchemy", which is a more general term that encompasses all the different forms of meditation practice. But for historical reasons, a specific class of meditation practices associated with physical movement became separated from the greater category of internal alchemy and was renamed, hence "qigong".

The first thing to understand is that internal alchemy was originally identified in contrast with "external alchemy" or waidan. This was the practice of trying to extend one's life through special diets and medicinal concoctions. No doubt some of this effort resulted in improved nutrition as people compared how different foods made them feel. Unfortunately, it also led to a lot of people poisoning themselves through actions like eating mercury and various poisonous plants. Eventually, external alchemy died out and was replaced by various meditational practices, which eventually ended up being call internal alchemy to differentiate it from external alchemy.

Fast forward to the Chinese Republic. At that time the government decided to encourage martial arts and other traditional forms of exercise in order to raise people's self-esteem and general physical well-being. One of the things they wanted to promote were a whole class of internal alchemy systems that were based on physical exercises. This included systems well-known today in the West, like taijiquan, but also other more obscure things like the "eight pieces of brocade" and the "five animal frolics". There was one "sticking point" for the Republican government, however. It was not in favour of encouraging traditional Chinese religions, as they believed that they were superstitions. As a result, they didn't want to promote these exercises as spiritual systems, but rather just as physical exercises. Part of this campaign, therefore, involved doing away with the old term, neidan, and replacing it with a new one, qigong.

....

Taijiquan is a bit of a special case. Many people do not realize that it is actually a martial art, but it is. This is an understandable misconception, as the overwhelming majority of people who practice it do so only as a form of gentle exercise. As such, they only do slow forms practice. But if you want to pursue it as a martial art all the various elements of any other fighting system can be pursued: tumbling, joint locks, kicks, throws, weapons, sparring, bag training, etc.

People who are "into" taijiquan will sometimes say that was created by the Daoist immortal Zhang Sanfeng after watching a fight between a crane and a snake. The more plausible story is that it was the developed by the Chen clan as its own fighting style. It was eventually adopted by Daoists as its own fighting style and along with Xingyi and Bagua became known as one of the three "Daoist" or "Wudang" "internal martial arts". This probably came about through rivalry with Buddhism---which had its own martial arts tradition

based on the Shaolin Temple. (The Daoist religion has a competitive
"me too" element that results in it trying to come up with its own
distinctive rituals and symbols that mirror those of Buddhism.)
Eventually, people modified it from a purely martial art into
something that could also be used for internal alchemy (qigong)
practice.

....

What people call qigong (ie: the eight pieces of brocade, the five
animal frolics, taijiquan, etc) is yet another venue for the elements
that I have identified previously with regard to sitting and forgetting,
and, holding onto the One. That is, the practice of learning intricate,
complex moving exercises forces the person doing them to learn how
to quiet their monkey mind. The taijiquan open-hand set, for example,
has over one hundred moves and if you get distracted it is very easy to
lose your place. In addition, many of the moves are very complicated
and are very hard to learn how to do well. If you start thinking about
things like what you want to eat for dinner or what happened at work,
you will lose your place in the set and forget how to do those complex
moves.

In addition, each of the moves requires very complex analysis of
how the geometry of your body works. Your knees have to be "just
so", you have to remember to relax so your centre of gravity will
drop, your posture has to be vertical, etc, etc. And in the midst of all
this complex thought, you have to remember to breath! And this
process never really ends. After regular practice for over thirty years, I
still learn new things about the taijiquan form on a very frequent
basis. This means that practicing the forms is an exploration of the
Dao (or the One.)

Doing Without Doing

I once had a co-worker with a hobby farm. He told me what a
huge hassle it was loading pigs onto a drover's truck in order to ship
them to market. The animals are obstinate, extremely strong, and his
barn lacked all the ramps and fencing that bigger barns use to channel
livestock onto trucks. One day he found a veterinary book on animal
handling. It suggested a method for moving pigs by simply placing a
bucket over their heads. Since the instinct of the hog is to back up out

of the bucket, the pig will invariable walk backwards and you can steer their direction of movement by pulling on the tail. He tried this method the next time he had some pigs to ship and said it worked like a charm. He simply put a plastic bucket over their heads, and they walked backwards up the ramp of the truck one at a time.

This was an example of the Daoist concept of "doing without doing", or, wei wu wei.

....

Our society is in love with brute force. We don't try to understand the subtle and complex elements of a problem, we just throw resources at it and try to pound it into submission. That's why our foreign policy never attempts to understand the various shades of grey in a country---we just blow things up. If people are taking drugs we don't try to understand why---we just declare "war" and start throwing them in jail. If we have traffic jams we don't try to rethink the way we plan cities---we just build bigger and bigger freeways. And if we have truculent animals that don't want to get onto a truck, most of us don't try to understand their behaviour---we just lose our temper and just try to beat them into submission.

It doesn't matter that this behaviour never works. That's because it really isn't about solving the issue, whether it be terrorism, drug abuse, traffic jams, or, obstinate pigs. Instead, we make it all about venting our frustrations and expressing our rage at a world that doesn't operate the way we want it to.

....

One of the exercises that one does when learning taijiquan as a martial art is "pushing hands" (tuishou).

This involves a process of two people holding each other's arms and going through a series of back and forth movements. The idea is that you learn how to sense each other's ability to maintain their balance. If you have achieved a certain degree of proficiency, you will gain the ability to gently push a person at exactly the right time and in exactly the right way to totally unbalance them. Similarly, you can also learn how to be "unsubstantial" so that when they try to push you, they find themselves pushing against empty space, which will also cause them lose their balance. And if you can unbalance the person, then they will be vulnerable to either a joint lock or being knocked over by a small application of force in the direction that they are already going. This is the principle behind the taijiquan saying that you can "deflect one thousand pounds with four ounces". This too is an example of "doing without doing".

....

In the middle of my city there is a beautiful area where the Speed and Eramosa rivers meet. Their banks have been naturalized and many people canoe, walk along trails, fish, and generally enjoy nature in an urban setting. Unfortunately, two major provincial roads come close to each other there. The official city plan at one time called for both of these roads to eventually connect through the construction of a road extension and large concrete bridge. This would have totally destroyed this jewel-like park.

The planning department understood what was at stake, but unfortunately, it was considered subservient to the city engineers. What this meant was that roads were not set out according to what the planning department wanted. Instead, the engineering department decided where roads would go, and planning's job was to accommodate people to what is ideal for the automobile. This meant that no matter how beautiful the park where the two rivers met, it would be destroyed in order to allow cars to move more smoothly through the city.

But the beautiful confluence of the two rivers is still there and no concrete bridge exists. Why? As my then city councillor explained it to me, the planning department realized that they could never win a direct fight with engineering. So instead of arguing against the road extension on aesthetic grounds, they instead set out to get the community on their side.

The local university found itself hosting a convention of timber framers. And as part of their activities, they offered to build a timber frame structure for the city if it would provide the land and materials. The planning department seized this opportunity and said that they wanted a timber frame pedestrian bridge over the Speed river where it meets up with the Eramosa. The result was an absolutely gorgeous covered bridge that offers the ideal place to view the confluence. Hundreds of local residents watched the official opening ceremony. People have been married on the bridge. It is one of the city's most important landmarks.

A few years later and the time came for the city to act on its engineering plan to connect the two roads and build the bridge. When the community realized that what was being proposed was a ugly concrete bridge filled with noisy traffic that would be running close to the timber frame pedestrian bridge, there was an instant insurrection. The Council had to face the political equivalent of pitchforks and torches. They quickly changed the plan and the two roads have never been connected. The planning department didn't openly defy the engineering department, but they won the struggle. That too is an example of doing without doing.

....

It's important to understand the principle. But that isn't enough. One has to be able to apply it. And to be able to do that, one has to develop the right way of looking at the world. People don't calmly choose to lash out and attack problems with brute force. Instead, they get into the habit of allowing their emotions to overwhelm their reason. Just like in push hands one learns how to feel another person's balance and learn to "deflect one thousand pounds with four ounces", so too through specific Daoist practices such as sitting and forgetting, and, holding onto the One, one learns how to remain calm and carefully observe the real situation before taking action. And if you do that, one will eventually gain the ability to do without doing.

"Chi" and Other Mysterious Things

If you read about Daoism you will inevitably come across language that mentions mysterious "energies" like "chi". For example, a quick Google search came up with this:

> *Central to Taoist world-view and practice is qi (chi). Qi is life-force -- that which animates the forms of the world. It is the vibratory nature of phenomena -- the flow and tremoring that is happening continuously at molecular, atomic and*

Actually, this isn't too far from an original Daoist view, as this quotation from the Nei-yeh suggests ("Chi" is translated as "vital essence"):

1 The vital essence of all things:

2 It is this that brings them to life.

3 It generates the five grains below

4 And becomes the constellated stars above.

5 When flowing amid the heavens and the earth

6 We call it ghostly and numinous.

7 When stored within the chests of human beings,

8 We call them sages.

(Original Tao: Inward Training (Nei-yeh), Verse 1, Harold D. Roth trans)

People with "New Age" tendencies will focus on this mysterious "energy" and talk about feeling chi flow through their bodies while doing tajiquan. Others will be concerned about the amount of "chi" in their food. Belief in chi becomes a sticking point for many people. Many people who call themselves Daoists see a belief in this occult phenomenon as being essential. On the other hand, many folks of a

more skeptical bent tend to see it as a "deal breaker" and dismiss
Daoism as just so much "wooo"---like belief in alien abductions or
pyramid power. I would suggest that both points of view are
understandable but somewhat naive.

....

I suspect that most people reading this book haven't thought
about this, but our collective understanding of the world advances
partially through our ability to invent new concepts to help us
organize our experiences in new ways. To understand this point,
consider the long history of "atoms". In the fifth century BC, a
philosopher named Democritus asked questions about what matter is
made up of. If you take a rock, for example, and grind it down into
smaller and smaller pieces, would you arrive at the "ultimately small"
piece of rock? Or would you be able to continue to break it into
smaller and smaller pieces forever? Democritus believed that there
had to be an "ultimate building block" of matter, which he called the
"atom".

Most folks would consider this just ridiculous speculation, but
once the idea was "out there", people eventually started thinking
about just how these tiny particles would work with one another. In
contrast to the atomic hypothesis, there also existed a competing one
based on four "elements": earth, air, fire and water. These were
substances that were defined by their "qualities"---earth is solid, air is
gaseous, fire is hot, and water is liquid. The atomic hypothesis argued
that these qualities were accidents in the arrangement of atoms, not
basic parts of the universe, whereas the "elemental" hypothesis
insisted that they were the basis of reality.

One particular divergence of the two hypotheses dealt with fire.
People who supported the elemental hypothesis suggested that there
was an elemental substance called "phlogiston" (from the Greek,
"burning up") that existed in things like wood. And when it burned,
this was being sucked out of it and absorbed by the air. This is why
wood ash weighs less than wood. And, a given volume of air can only
absorb so much phlogiston, which is why fire goes out we put it in a
totally enclosed space. Experiments caused problems with the
phlogiston hypothesis, however. For example, some substances, such

as metals, gain weight when they burn, which would suggest something else is taking place than the hypothesis would suggest.

After a series of experiments, the atomic hypothesis described combustion as a process where heat is given off by the combination of one set of atoms with oxygen. In that hypothesis the fact that metals gain weight from combustion whereas wood loses it is explained. The difference is that wood is largely made of carbon. When carbon combines with oxygen through combustion, the resulting molecule, CO_2, is a gas. The gas drifts away from the ash, which means the ash weighs less than the original wood. In contrast metals burn by combining with oxygen to create molecules that are a solid. This means that metal ash weights more than the original metal---because you have added the weight of the oxygen.

The important point I'm trying to raise is that for human knowledge to grow, we need to create concepts that allow us to have an intelligent conversation about specific issues. In the case of fire, Democritus' speculation about the ultimate nature of reality was helpful in getting chemists thinking beyond the old idea of there being four elements that are qualities instead of substances. Even "phlogiston" is a useful concept in that it stepped even beyond the idea that fire was just an element by trying to describe a mechanism behind combustion. The conversation between the two hypotheses allowed chemists like Lavoisier to create experiments that would eventually discover and describe a specific type of atom, which was called "oxygen". Without Democritus' original speculation and the resulting concept of the "atom", modern chemistry might have found it much harder to emerge as the scientific discipline we know today.

....

"Chi" is an idea that was created at roughly the same time in human history that Democritus was talking about "atoms". I am arguing that as such it was a useful hypothesis that allowed people to talk about mysterious aspects of life. It was an attempt to answer to the following sorts of questions: "What is the difference between life and death?", "Why are some people healthy and strong, whereas others are sick and weak?", "Why are some people socially influential and others 'no-bodies'?", and, "What are these strange feelings in my body when I do certain things?". The answer to all of these questions was "chi".

A dead body can look exactly the same as a live one, but it lacks "chi". Weak people are either "low on chi" or they have a "chi blockage" in their body. A "sage" or "realized man" can instantly command the attention of other people because he is filled with "powerful chi". And when you have strange feelings in various parts of the body, it's because you can feel the "chi" flowing through it. Ancients all over the world talked about this sort of thing. The Greeks used the term "pneumos", the Indians "prana", the Arabs, "baraka", and so on.

What was happening is the result of a very simple problem that is basic to the way all of us think. The ancients didn't have a way of thinking about "processes", so they had a conceptual bias towards thinking about complex activities as "things". We still have this bias now. That's why we identify a lot of verbs as nouns. Take for instance a sporting event like a foot race. People refer to specific races like the Boston Marathon, but ultimately what is happening is several human beings are running along a course to see who is fastest. This an activity, not a thing.

We also make other conceptual errors by wildly over-generalizing groups of people. For example, we say "America declared war on Iraq". But the geographic entity known as the USA didn't invade. Nor did the entire people collectively decide to attack. In fact, what happened was a coalition of influential individuals who found themselves in control of the machinery of government in America for a short period of time declared war on Iraq. As a matter of fact people rarely use this sort of phrasing because it is wordy. But saying things like that is a lot more accurate than common parlance. And people get themselves into a great many problems by not remembering that this is just a type of short hand. For example, outsiders routinely blame the entire American people for the decisions of their ruling class. Many terrorists seem motivated to attack all Americans for the crimes it's government has committed across the world---but precious few of the people who get killed have had anything to do with those atrocities or would even support them if anyone had asked their opinion in the first place. Similarly, some Americans want to blame and punish all Muslims or Arabs for the actions of a very small number of terrorists.

These are what modern philosophers call "category mistakes". They are manifestations of a flaw in reasoning where you take one type of concept with its own distinct set of rules for understanding it and confuse it with another type that has a very different set. Let's consider yet another example---one that is less laden with emotion. The words "University of Guelph" denote a conceptual grouping of very different things: a history, a legal entity, a geographic location, a collection of scholars, students and support staff, and so on. Yet someone could walk from the Arts building to the Library to the Science Complex and ask, "Yes, but where is the University?" The problem is that the grammar of our language seems to imply that a "university" is a physical object, when it isn't. The university campus is a physical entity, but not the university itself, which is more a conceptual agglomeration of various things---some physical and some not.

This is the same problem that confronts us when we talk about "chi". What we perceive as "life" in a person, for example, is not a "thing", but rather a process---the eyes move, the chest breathes in and out, the heart beats, etc. And when someone feels "chi" moving in their body it could be any number of things, such as hormones moving through the nervous system. The ancients didn't have a clue about how complex our bodies or the world around them was. They'd never heard of "nerves", "cells", "hormones", "conditioned reflexes", or any of the other gazillion things that modern science has revealed about how our bodies work. But they had to start somewhere, and where they started was by trying to explain things through some sort of subtle substance that they labelled "chi".

....

When different groups approach statements in the old books about "chi" most of them come from one of two perspectives. They can blindly accept them as "ancient Chinese wisdom", or, dismiss them out-of-hand as "so much New Age bosh". In both cases I suspect that this is caused by not understanding how important conceptual sophistication is to the understanding the world around us. Both groups would benefit from asking themselves the following questions:

"Do I think that the ancient Daoist masters were Gods who understood everything?" or, "Do I think they were total morons that couldn't possibly have anything worthwhile to teach us?" If you answer in the affirmative to either, then I have nothing more to say to you. But if you answer in the negative, then you have to admit that no matter how wise these guys were, they were labouring under the limitations of the culture they inhabited. At that point it is possible to look at the statements made in their books and understand how they could be improved upon by people who have had the benefit of thousands of years in cultural progress. IMHO, this should make New Agers a little more willing to listen to people who take issue with their cherished theories and Skeptics a little less willing to dismiss ancient ideas totally out-of-hand. Consider the following quotation---.

> *"Bernard of Chartres used to compare us to dwarfs perched on the shoulders of giants. He pointed out that we see more and farther than our predecessors, not because we have keener vision or greater height, but because we are lifted up and borne aloft on their gigantic stature."*

(attributed to John of Salisbury in the Wikipedia)

Religious Daoism

I started out this book by emphasizing that what I am describing is Daoism as a practical philosophy. At this point I should mention that this is in opposition to Daoism as a religion. Most Westerners don't even know that there is such a thing. Oddly enough, I've found that people really have a hard time recognizing something that they don't expect. For example, I used to identify myself as a "Daoist" and tried to live something like a religious Daoist and found that even friends simply couldn't wrap their heads around this idea. One fellow got it into his head that I was a Muslim and I could never get him to understand that I am not. Another called me a Buddhist for much the same reason. A Benedictine nun friend had the idea that I had just made up all this Daoism stuff. Well, I didn't. In China and amongst the Chinese diaspora there are temples, and, "priests" (daoshi) of a religion known as "Daoism".

....

I'm not an expert, but from my reading on the subject it seems the religion came from a lot of different sources. As I mentioned above, there appears to have been an oral tradition that created foundational texts such as the **Nei-Yeh** and the **Dao De Jing**. This tradition also created meditation techniques like sitting and forgetting, holding onto the One, and, internal alchemy.

In addition, there was another stream called "Chinese folk religion". This is a part of the cultural inheritance of ordinary Chinese society. It includes things like a pantheon of various gods and immortals such as the Jade Emperor, the Queen Mother of the West, the Ghost King, General Kwan, the God of Longevity, and so on. (When you go into a Chinese-owned business in the West you will often see an altar to one or several of these folk gods.)

In addition, there are shamanist traditions that involve things like the "sand oracle". This involves a specialist who is "possessed" by one of the gods and who answers questions put to the her by writing with a chopstick on a pan of sand. (I was told that the fellow who travelled from Hong Kong to Canada to set up the Fung Loy Kok temple and who initiated me, immigrated on the advice of a sand oracle.)

Yet another element in the creation of the Daoist religion was a rebellion by the exploited lower classes of Chinese society. This was the "yellow turban rebellion" which started in the year 184 and lasted until the year 205 CE. It was organized by the "Five Pecks of Rice Daoists", led by the "Celestial Master". (The "five pecks of rice" refers to a tax that members were expected to pay into a communal bank and which was used to help the poor and support collective undertakings.) After the rebellion was quashed by the armies of Imperial China (part of the campaign is described in the Chinese classic novel Three Kingdoms) the movement became more religiously focused and lives on today as one of the two major daoist sects: Zheng Yi Dào, or, "the Way of Orthodox Unity". Orthodox Daoism tends to be based on a priesthood that minister to local communities of followers. They hold public rituals, organize charitable activity, perform exorcisms and healing ceremonies, and, generally act something like pastors in rural protestant Christian communities.

········

The other major sect of Daoism, the Quanzhen or "the Way of Completeness and Truth", was founded about a thousand years after Orthodox Daoism by Wang Chongyang. The legend is that Wang met three Daoist immortals in a tavern and they taught him secret meditation techniques, which he went on to perfect while living many years of intense practice, first in a tomb and then in a hut. After this period, he adopted seven followers (who became famous as the "Seven Daoist Masters" of Chinese folklore), who then went on to found seven major Daoist sects. The most famous of these disciples, Changchun zi, caught the ear of the Mongol Emperor Genghis Khan, who granted him land in the Imperial Capital of Beijing, which eventually became one of the greatest sites in Daoism, the White Cloud Temple.

The Quanzhen school grew in something of a tension with Buddhism, which had come from India after the creation of Orthodox Daoism. Chinese culture was generally opposed to celibacy and monasticism, which is reflected in the teachings of the Celestial Master, who encouraged his followers to marry and integrate themselves into the community. In contrast, Buddhism has always encouraged its followers to isolate themselves from mainstream society. By the time of Wang Chongyang Buddhism had become very popular in China, and the obvious conclusion would be that it influenced the development of Quanzhen Daoism---which favours monasticism, just like Buddhism.

········

In addition, I understand that in the 19th century there were popular spiritual movements amongst the lower classes which taught the unity of all religions and the importance of charity and mutual aid. Unfortunately, the Communist Party of China saw these groups as competitors and ruthlessly suppressed them in mainland China. The temple that I was initiated into, the Fung Loy Kok, was an offshoot of a Hong Kong organization, the Yuen Yuen Institute, that embodied these ideals. This adds yet another element "to the mix".

··········

I suspect that the majority of people who read this book will consider all religions to be not much more than superstitious nonsense. To a certain extent I do too, but I have to offer one caveat. To understand it, I think people have to realize that while all people may be created equal, they are not created the same.

One of the "basic operating assumptions" that all human beings work with is the idea that each of us has a similar way of experiencing the world. When I see a rose, I assume that someone else sees much the same thing. But in point of fact, it is very difficult to know if this is actually true. I can point at what I see and tell someone else that it is a "rose", which will lead to her using the same word whenever she sees the same thing again. But I have no real way of telling if she sees a soft, red, nest of petals. For all I know, she might be seeing what I would experience as a hard, blue, pile of crystals.

If this sounds absurd, consider the fact that a certain percentage of the population suffers from an affliction known as colour blindness. I went to school with a guy who simply could not tell the difference between green and red because both looked the same to him. This caused a problem for him on his family's farm because it meant that he couldn't tell the difference in ripeness for some types of fruit. His experience of a rose is significantly different than mine.

Now let's push this issue even further. There is also a very small percentage of people who have something called "synesthesia", which means that they experience one type of sense in ways that most people associate with another sense altogether. A sound, for example, may have a colour. This is so alien to me that I simply cannot understand what it would be like. In my experience, only visual objects have colour. Yet we don't see sound, we only hear it---so how could it have a colour?

Let's go totally wild. There are cases of individuals who have been profoundly blind since birth yet they have learned how to live much like normal people by developing the ability to echo locate like bats. One example I saw on YouTube has developed this ability to the point where he is able to ride a bicycle and shoot hoops with a basketball. He does it just like a bat---he makes clicking noises and uses the echoes he hears to create a mental three dimensional image that allows him to navigate the world around him.

There are other examples. People who become chess masters often show off by playing multiple games of chess in their heads. This isn't a "fluke", but rather a by-product of developing the ability to recognize the patterns in play that define a master instead of an ordinary player. Another example is a random pattern autostereogram (look it up on Wikipedia.) These are pictures that look like nothing at all until a person's brain learns the "trick" of decoding the information---but once you do, a full-fledged, three-dimensional picture "jumps" up at you off the page. The point I am trying to make is that contrary to naive assumptions, people do not all experience the world in the same way. And for some people religion is all total "bosh", whereas others experience something incredibly important.

Part of this is a question of emotion. People aren't just thinking beings, but also feeling ones. And for many people, religion is about feeling deeply about a specific God. I've never been able to understand the strong feeling that some Christians have about their Gods (Jesus, the Father, the Saints), but then again my childhood experiences were not conducive to feeling deeply about other family members. (Union meetings where people talk about "brothers" and "sisters" also leave me cold.)

What I do have more sympathy towards are people who claim to have had religious experiences.

> *When God came into my teenage or college bedroom in that way, unasked and unmistakable, the next morning I would wake up changed. I'd go out into the world and give away everything I could. Wouldn't drive past a broken-down car without stopping to help, was kind and grateful even with my parents, couldn't stop singing, built houses for poor people, gave secret gifts to my friends, things like that. Sometimes it lasted for weeks; once, when I was in my early twenties, it*

I've had experiences like the ones Dombek describes, which is
why I have some sympathy for them. I've also had them associated
with numinous dreams where I met with figures from Daoist
mythology---the Goddess of Mercy and the Ghost King.

People who've never had this sort of experience say that they
simply cannot understand what people are talking about. (I suspect
that a significant fraction of these people has actually had something
like this happen to them, but it scared them so much that they refuse
to admit it. But I have to take most of them on their word, after all can
we really know what it's like to be in someone else's skin?)

Of course, some folks will probably just dismiss this as
something akin to a manic episode and chalk all religious experiences
to low grade psychiatric illness. As someone with more than my fair
share of exposure to people with obvious psychiatric disorders, my
humble opinion is that this is a facile response. The line between
madness and sanity is far more ambiguous than that point of view
would suggest. We create a socially-sanctioned definition and discard
many important elements of ordinary consciousness in creating the
"received version" of what it means to be a human being. My opinion
is in line with that of Temple Grandin (the famous autistic professor
of animal science.) I once heard her interviewed on the CBC where
she suggested that human consciousness exists on a continuum and
both autism and bipolar disorder are extremes of very useful human
tendencies. Remove all autism from the human population and you
will have removed all the scientists, mathematicians and engineers
too. And take away bipolar disorder, and there would be no more
artists. I won't hazard a guess about what is involved in religious
experiences, but perhaps if we removed the ability to love God we
would also remove the ability to love anything or anyone.

....

Another thing to remember about organized religion is that it is a way of unifying a population of people around a central theme or set of ideals. When people see a ritual they are not arguing amongst themselves in a search for some sort of clear and precise truth. Instead, they are doing one or many of several different things. They might be enjoying music and art, or, they might be feeling good about being part of a community experience, or, they may be feeling nostalgic about past experiences of a similar sort, or, they might be having a profoundly emotional experience triggered by feelings associated with specific symbols. The feeling and ideas aroused by the experience may vary from person to person, indeed, they might be totally contradictory. But because the ideas and emotions raised remain on the theoretical level instead of being explicitly articulated, there is no opportunity for people to realize this fact, so the event brings them together instead of pushing them apart. For example, a given ritual might be attended by an artist who appreciates the beautiful calligraphy on the altar; an old woman who is reminded about the village festivals of her youth; a young mother who is happy to be surrounded by her extended family; children who are happy for all the noise, gaudy clothes, and, good food; and, a young intellectual who views the public worship of the Gods as a way of connecting to the long history of the nation. All the same things can be said about a Roman Catholic mass.

Contrast this with what happens when a philosopher tries to get people to clearly articulate their beliefs about a contentious subject. People who thought that they were in agreement usually find out that they believe very different things. Tempers often flare up. And the community divides. Ritual unites a community---discursive reasoning divides it. This is why ancient Athens put Socrates to death and why I can seem to be a total jerk at a party. But the great value of discursive reasoning is that it deflates superstition, expands human knowledge, and, separates fact from opinion. It offers progress in place of comfort. I understand the appeal of religion, but ultimately I know that I am more of a philosopher than a believer. This is why I ultimately rejected religious Daoism and am writing this book. But it doesn't mean that I cannot understand the appeal. I would hope that all those rationalists who read this book will at least try to understand this point too.

A lot of people make a big deal about so-and-so being a "Master" or even a "Grand Master". At best, this is based on allegiance to a specific school or teaching. At worst it manifests itself in the silly school-yard mentality of "my master can whip your master". Most of this can be ultimately traced to the human predisposition towards tribalism. It's also a manifestation of the idea that "Old Tymey" things are better than "New Fangled", and that "secret hidden teachings" have been handed down through generations of mystic teachers. Some of this is understandable as people need to have some respect for the experience of their teachers and also have to take some stuff "on faith" before they gain enough personal experience to be able to separate the wheat from the chaff. Unfortunately, far too many people take this impulse way too far and as a result folks---both teachers and students---fall into the trap of "guru worship".

Guru worship is a really bad idea. For students, it dramatically diminishes their ability to think for themselves. As a result, they stop being critical not only about what the actions of their teacher, but also of what they are learning. Beyond all the unhealthy interpersonal dynamics, this dramatically reduces one's ability to learn. Just think about how well the average high school student could learn something like math or chemistry if they lost the ability to critically evaluate what they were doing. They'd be fine at copying the work that the teacher wrote on the blackboard, but they'd be useless at applying the theory to a particular new example.

That's because they need to look at a novel application of general theory by looking at it from different points of view. "What if I?---No, that won't work because---." The ability to think critically is like a muscle. If you stop using it in one part of your life, it atrophies in all the others. Perhaps this is why in any given class the very best students tend to be smart asses, whereas the "goody two-shoes" are usually mediocre. This is because as a student you don't really know enough to be able to tell the difference between what you think the "Master" wants you to learn and what she may actually want you to learn. The only way to tell the difference is to critically evaluate what you think you were taught and if you find a problem, take that back to her. And this process not only looks like you are questioning the value of a teaching, it always holds the possibility that that's exactly what's going on. This is a scary prospect for someone who is worshipping a guru.

Teachers who assume the rank of "worshipped guru" also suffer. This happens because almost inevitably they end up "believing their own advertising". No matter how much you try to remind yourself that you really aren't the enlightened, groovy, saint that your students think you are, inevitably you start taking their adulation for granted. At best this means that you will stop learning from your own mistakes and the insights of others. At worst you exploit your followers and start collecting Rolls Royces and "cute young things". So truth be told, not only should students run from teachers who call themselves "Masters", but teachers should run from students who call them that too.

....

"The man makes the art, the art doesn't make the man," sums up one part of the problem pretty well. Daoism is not about creating a specific type of person that is an immediately recognizable "known quantity"---like army basic training. Instead, it is about engaging with an alternative viewpoint of life in order to develop your best qualities as an individual. This creates a problem with people who have an idealized vision of "Mastery" because it actually encourages them to totally submerge their individuality to the absolute, grooviness of the guru they worship. That's pretty much the exact opposite of what Daoism is all about.

....

Sometimes people come up with lineage charts (like the pedigree charts that animal breeders use) that link teachers who were taught by other teachers, who were taught by other teachers back to the totally, ultimately grooviest teachers. For example, I have a copy of one of these things that links the guys who initiated me into a temple all the way back to Laozi and Gautama Buddha. Of course, this is total poppy-cock. Historians have pointed out that these sorts of transmission chains fall apart when you look at them in detail. There are always gaps in "transmission" from one person to another. The role they serve, in actual fact, is to raise the credibility of the guy in front of you and to stop you from thinking for yourself. After all,

"what I am saying comes all the way from Laozi and the Buddha---
who are you to question me?"

....

The only way in which being called a "Master" makes sense is
the same way it is used with regard to the skilled trades or university
degrees. Traditionally, a "Master" craftsman was the culmination of a
process that started with an apprentice and moved through
journeyman. The journeyman was someone who has passed their
apprenticeship and was therefore qualified to work on a jobsite
without any supervision. But they weren't qualified to teach
apprentices or run their own shop. The difference comes down to how
deep one's theoretical understanding of the craft had become. Part of
the process involved having to create a "master work" that showed
that a person understood their craft so well that they could design and
craft something spectacular that is very different from anything else
that had been done before. This theoretical understanding was
necessary for the Master's ability to articulate and explain the craft to
customers and future generations of apprentices alike.

In a similar manner, the "Master's" and "Doctorate" degrees at
university were originally designated to identify people who were
qualified to teach at the university level. Originally, the Master's
degree was supposed to be for people who specialized in teaching and
the Doctorate for those who were more research oriented. More
recently, the former has become a stepping stone towards the latter---
although you will still find people teaching at universities with just a
Masters degree and people in Phd programs without a Master's.
Again, the difference between post-graduate and baccalaureate
degrees comes down to the ability of a person to produce a "Master
work" (ie a thesis) and the ability to teach future generations.

....

To become a Master electrician or to get a Master's degree from a
university there is a formal process that results in a piece of paper that
has a certain value all over the world. For example, I have a Master's
degree from the University of Guelph. Since Canadian public
universities are considered quite good by the community of scholars,

this degree is recognized all over the world. In the same way, a Master's electrician license has a certain objective value.

No similar ranking system exists for "Daoist Masters". There is a system in China for ranking people at Daoist Temples, but the fact of the matter is that very high ranking officials are appointed by the government, and they appoint the others---which means that the Communist Party of China has the ultimate say in who is who in official Daoist circles. This situation has pretty much always been the case, as the big Temples like White Cloud or Wudang Shan were important cultural treasures and as such of importance to the government---be it Mongol, Han, Manchu, or, Communist. Moreover, the Daoist world was split into different sects: Quanzhen, Zhengyi Dao, Maoshan, and many others. "Credentials" issued at one school had about as much value as a theology degree from Bob Jones University has at the Vatican. (At this point in time the Communist government has forced all different types of religious Daoists to register either as Quanzhen or Zhengyi styles. This is more than a little bit of a "procrustean bed".)

Ultimately, the people who identify someone as a Daoist "Master" are the people who are willing to call him one. That's why some folks go to great lengths to promote themselves as "Masters". They invent lineage charts, talk about mysterious groovy guys that have taught them and handed down mysterious "secret teachings", wear outlandish clothing, etc. This is really campaigning for students to vote for their ascension to the position of groovy Master. Once you get a certain degree of support you can get your already existing supporters to do some or all of the campaigning for you, which makes the promotion a little less obvious. If you really hit the jackpot, you can create an entire institution with paid staff and buildings who can continue the promotion even after you are dead and gone. That's how a Temple gets built.

But for anyone who is interested in learning Daoism it all boils down to "yah pays your money, yah makes your choices." People who like being groovy Masters don't like to admit this fact, but that is really what it's all about.

Daoists who are of a "New Age" or religious orientation will often talk about "Immortals" or "Enlightened Sages" who have either conquered death or at least have manifested magical powers. This idea has existed for a long time, as it stems from the Shamanistic roots of the broad movement. But as a practical philosophy I would suggest that people need not accept that there are such things as magical powers or immortality in order to be a "real Daoist".

So let's look at how one of the key Daoist thinkers, Zhuangzi, viewed life and death.

> *Master Chuang's wife died. When Master Hui went to offer his condolences, he found Master Chuang lolling on the floor with his legs sprawled out, beating a basin and singing.*
>
> *"She lived together with you," said Master Hui, "raised your children, grew old, and died. It's enough that you do not wail for her, but isn't it a bit much for you to be beating on a basin and singing?"*
>
> *"Not so," said Master Chuang. "When she first died, how could I of all people not be melancholy? But I reflected on her beginning and realized that originally she was unborn. Not only was she unborn, originally she had no form. Not only did she have no form, originally she had no vital breath. Intermingling with nebulousness and blurriness, a transformation occurred and there was vital breath; the vital breath was transformed and there was form; the form was transformed and there was birth; now there has been another transformation and she is dead. This is like the progression of the four seasons---from spring to autumn, from winter to summer. There she sleeps blissfully in an enormous chamber. If I were to have*

followed her weeping and wailing, I think it would have been out of keeping with destiny, so I stopped."

(Zhuangzi, "Outer Chapters", "Ultimate Joy", Sect 2, Mair trans.)

There is an important insight in Daoism that involves life and death. But it isn't a secret that only very groovy people are allowed to hear. Instead, its one of those insights that is relatively easy to find, but only a certain type of person is willing to listen to.

Master Lieh was on a journey and was having a meal by the side of the road. There he saw a hundred-year-old skull. He pulled away the weeds and pointed at it, saying, "Only you and I know that you have never died and that you have never lived. Are you truly distressed? Am I truly happy?"

(**Zhuangzi**, "Outer Chapters", "Ultimate Joy", Sect 6, Mair trans.)

Liezi can say that the skull has "never died" and "never lived". That's because human beings don't really exist. They are actually only theoretical abstractions. All of us die, and we could end up dried bones on a roadside. But is the bone the man? Hardly. Indeed, is the infant the man? When you die, there is no "you" left to give a hang about being dead. No more than there was anyone to be concerned about before you were born.

And think about this. Modern psychology has proved beyond a doubt that what we call "memory" is to a large degree fiction. Our minds aren't tape recorders that keep everything on a permanent record. Instead, they are like data compression files that record a few salient elements of the past and then use our imagination to reconstruct it when required according to various protocols. This explains the phenomenon of "false memory syndrome". It also explains why eye-witness testimony is so notoriously unreliable. What we remember is to a disconcertingly large extent fiction! What we experience of life are odd fleeting moments of self-awareness, an anticipation of what the future may bring, plus a largely fictional understanding of the past.

Look carefully at life and you don't find individuals that have lives, let alone people who are immortal. Instead, what you find is a process.

> *In seeds there are germs. When they are found in water they become filaments. When they are found at the border of water and land they become algae. When they are found at the border of water and land they become plantain. When the plantain is found in fertile soil it becomes crow's foot. The crow's foot's roots become scarab grubs and its leaves become butterflies. The butterflies soon evolve into insects that are born beneath the stove. They have the appearance of exuviae and are called "house crickets". After a thousand days the house crickets become birds called "dried surplus bones." The spittle of the dried surplus bones becomes a misty spray and the misty spray becomes mother of vinegar. Midges are born from mother of vinegar: yellow whirligigs are born from fetid wine; blind gnats are born from putrid slime bugs. When goat's-queue couples with bamboo that has not shooted for a long time, they produce greenies. The greenies produce panthers; panthers produce horses; horses produce men; and men return to enter the wellsprings of nature. The myriad things all come out from the wellsprings and all re-enter the wellsprings.*

(**Zhuangzi,** "Outer Chapters", "Ultimate Joy", sect 7, Mair trans.)

Zhuangzi is having fun with the science of the day, but the point he is trying to make is that if you look at life what you see is a complex booming, buzzing series of changes. That is the Dao and the Dao is all there is. We tie ourselves in knots worrying about entities that are mere intellectual abstractions.

There are no "immortals" because there really are no "mortals". There is just the endless series of transformations, which Daoists call "the Dao". A "Master"---if you want to use the term---is simply someone who's figured this out to some extent. Sometimes they can find someone what wants to hear what they have to say, and sometimes that person actually understands what they are being told. But usually no one wants to hear what a "Master" has to say, so she just goes on with her life. There is another term that is sometimes used instead---one that I like much better than "Master" or "Immortal": "Realized Man". Someone who has figured out the Dao is a "Realized Man"---but mostly he is just another guy who has gained some insight into what life is really like.

....

On a more practical note, it is important to understand why it is that people might think that some Daoists actually became immortal or developed super-human powers. At various times in human history the average lifespan has been a lot shorter than what we take for granted now. Consider a time in ancient China when life wasn't very good. Peasants lived short lives because they wore their bodies out by hard, brutal labour. And wealthier people who lived in cities tended to die because of the diseases that were endemic because of bad sanitation. (It's only in the 19th century that the population of large cities became self-reproducing. Before that, disease deaths always out-paced births and to keep the population stable there had to be a constant flow of people from rural areas moving in to balance this out. Consider the fact that even Queen Victoria's husband, Prince Albert, died in a cholera epidemic!)

Contrast this with the life of a hermit in some wilderness area. Isolated from other people, he wouldn't have been exposed to infectious diseases. And not being a peasant, he was able to avoid damaging his body through over work. Finally, being someone concerned about long life, he would have tried to have a varied diet and balanced exercise. Some of these folks probably would have been able to live to the immense age of seventy or eighty years! In a world where most people are dead by age forty and at sixty you are a very old man, someone in their eighties would be considered a magical being! Now if someone saw one of these rare oldsters, they would have talked about it. A game of "telephone" would have ensued and before long, people would have heard stories of mysterious "ancient immortals" who inhabit the mountains.

Similarly, if someone spends their time looking at the world around them and thinking about what they see, they might have noticed some interesting facts. Pass these facts onto other disciples, and eventually a body of "magical powers" can get built up. For example, for centuries religious leaders have "wowed" naive followers through ritual fire walking. Well, it turns out that even though glowing coals are very hot, they have a very poor rate of conductivity. This means that if someone walks barefoot on them, the perspiration on the soles of the feet are able to protect them from damage. (If someone put an iron railway spike in the fire---which has excellent conductive power---their feet would be terribly burned.). Now that people understand the science, fire walking is routinely used at conventions of scientific skeptics and business training seminars where there is no attempt to suggest magic is involved.

This is what my teacher used to call a "circus trick". There are lots and lots of them and they are all based on either scientific principles that are poorly understood, or, out-and-out fraud. For ancients they were an excellent way of "gulling the rubes" in the neighbourhood of the hermitage. At the very best this sort of thing would teach them to leave you alone. At the worst, it was a way of getting some economic support for your lifestyle. (Many "hermits" actually had people providing food and clothing---some even had servants.) Again, something unexplained would probably be spread through word of mouth and get exaggerated as it went from person to person. A circus trick eventually became a miracle.

....

Most people really want to believe in there being "something more to life". When they contemplate the horror and misery that many of us have to live through, they want there to be some sort of redress or balance in some future existence. Others find themselves in such drab, boring lives that they want to believe that this is just an illusion that covers something far more interesting. But these hopes don't make any sense at all---even if we assume that they have some basis in fact. For example, even if there was such a thing as reincarnation it really doesn't make our lives here and now any better. This is because it doesn't really matter if in a previous life I was the Emperor of China if I cannot remember it. And even if I did, the memory would only serve as a contrast to the blah, humdrum quality of my present 21st century existence. The same can be said about going to heaven after death, which is ultimately not much more than a specific type of reincarnation. As for there being a secret, amazing reality hiding behind normal existence, as Bishop Berkley pointed out, "esse est percipi", or, "the essence of something is how we perceive it". That is to say that if something "walks like a duck, quacks like a duck, swims like a duck", etc---we should just accept that it is a duck instead of hypothesising a lot of other things that no one can sense. And, as I wrote before, if the past is mostly imagination and the future mere anticipation, we only exist for the fleeting instant of awareness called "NOW!". And if we only exist now, what does it mean to say that you live a long, short, or, immortal life?

Realised men do not know any tremendously groovy things that are hidden the rest of us. Instead, they are people who have the courage to see and accept the truths that are in front of all of us all the time.

The "Unhewn Log"

Another core Daoist idea is that of "unhewn log" or pu. This is the idea that all things, even human beings, have an innate nature that is perverted when it is forced to conform to external control. Civilization---especially in the form of Confucian ceremonies, rules, and, rituals---twists and perverts people's essential nature. Although the ancient Daoists had no theory of "socio-biology", I suspect that they would agree that there is a basic, ideal sort of life built into our human genes that civilization often distorts. Daoist literature not only complains about how society twists our lives, it also paints visions of a sort of ancient utopia where people can live their lives in harmony with their essential nature.

Zhuangzi, "Horses Hooves", Mair, trans.

Modern people do not live lives governed by the strict rules of filial piety and decorum of Confucianism, but we are hemmed-in by other regulations that are in many ways even worse. We live our lives based on clock time, which means that for many people arriving at work as little as five minutes late can result in a gut-wrenching inter-personal conflict with their boss. We not only don't live in harmony with the "birds and the beasts", our society is engaged in a genocidal war against them. In many ways, our competitive "growth at all costs", capitalist lifestyle is every bit as constrained as the one lived in a Confucianist house-hold. We have merely traded a domineering mother-in-law and over-bearing father for a boss and the gnawing fear of unemployment. The need to kowtow before an altar of the ancestors has been replaced by the need to feign enthusiasm for the company vision statement. Henry David Thoreau's belief that "The mass of men lead lives of quiet desperation, and go to the grave with the song still in them." is just as true today as it was in his time---and even when Zhuangzi put pen to paper.

I personally do not believe that human beings are as defined by our "essential nature" as the idea of the unhewn log would suggest, but I do agree with Zhuangzi that there are some ways of living that work better for people than others. It is a bald truth that our civilization has painted itself into a corner and cannot go back to the utopian vision of small village life that the Daoists painted. (I suspect that this was no longer possible even in Zhuangzi's time.) But through social and political activism it is possible to change our current civilization to one that is in harmony with the best qualities of human beings. We can incrementally move towards a society more in harmony with nature, less competitive, and, more free. By holding onto the ideal of the unhewn log, we will have a star to guide us on that journey.

The Useless Tree

We live in a society that "knows the price of everything and the value of nothing"---to quote Oscar Wilde. We only value something insofar as it has utility for someone else. Indeed, sometimes we only recognize a thing's existence if it can be reduced to a number and used by an accountant to manipulate the "bottom line". Indeed, that phrase has become synonymous in everyday conversation and political discourse as meaning "the ultimate criteria" for making any decision. This is why we build "brutalist" buildings and suburban sprawl---they are cheap to build so we create a fake aesthetic to justify their form.

In fact, the modern "utilitarian" design of our cities is tremendously inefficient for the people who live in them. The "utility" only refers to the people who make money off building them. Giant, ugly skyscrapers and endless sprawl are very profitable to developers, but they force the people who live and work in them to spend far too much of their lives commuting huge distances to go from soul-less homogenity to ugly conformity. This is hardly efficient for the people who live these lives or for the environment that has to soak up the enormous ecological footprint.

Sir Motley of Southunc made an excursion to the Hillock of Shang. There he saw an unusual tree so

Zhuangzi, "The Human World", part 5, Mair trans.

Many years ago I worked as a janitor in a major department store.
Once a year, the major share holders would come through in an
inspection tour. When this happened, our foreman asked us to "give it
our all" to make the store as clean as possible. We really worked hard
and after the tour the store manager came to us, shook our hands, and
told us that the shareholders had informed him that his store was the
cleanest one in the country. The next week we had our hours were cut.
The store was obviously too clean, and our extra work resulted in a
significant decrease in pay. I learned a very important lesson that day.
When you work you do not work for your employer or your
customer---you work for yourself.

Institutions, abstractions, ideologies, none of them have any
value in and of themselves. These are merely means to an end.
People, nature, beautiful works of art, these are what have intrinsic
value. The truly valuable are never useful, because the concept of
utility is always directed outwards and never inward. In your life
always remember that you are more important than the profit that any
employer or customer wishes to extract from you. And you are also
more important than any institutional goal that the government,
political party, or, religious body asks you to sacrifice towards. Being

78

useless means that you will never be used. If you remember this, you stand a greater chance of not being personally abused.

Moreover, if you remember this fact you also stand a much greater chance of not finding yourself abusing others in pursuit of some external goal. Remembering that you have your own intrinsic value as a human being is the first step to remembering that everyone else has a similar value.

Sentimentality

1. Heaven and earth are not humane (jen),

They treat the ten thousand beings as straw dogs (ch'u kou).

The sage is not humane (jen),

He treats the hundred families as straw dogs (ch' kou).

2. Between heaven and earth,

How like a bellows (t'o yo) it is!

Empty and yet inexhaustible,

Moving and yet it pours out ever more.

3. By many words one's reckoning (shu) is exhausted.

It is better to abide by the center (shou chung).

(Chapter Five, Laozi, Ellen Chen trans.)

"Jen" is a key Confucian virtue that suggests that people have an innate desire or drive to help one another. While not universally expressed, it is something that is potentially in all human beings if they try. Usually this word is translated as "sentimental" but Chen has translated it as "humane". This is an important point, because the chapter becomes a lot easier to take if you think of it as a rejection of saccharine sentimentality. It is much harsher than that, however, Laozi is saying that the universe is totally indifferent to human suffering. It might be that some, or even all, people have jen, but the world certainly doesn't.

He implies this by saying that every creature (ie "the ten thousand beings"), every human being ("the hundred families") are just "straw dogs". Straw dogs were cheap representations of the animals that used to be used as sacrifices during religious rituals. (They were the same as the "Hell Money" that you can find in any Chinese grocery and which is burned as a sacrifice during various festivals.) Straw dogs are simply worthless objects that are destroyed in the place of things that are actually worth too much to be wasted.

Contrast this Daoist statement with the lyrics of this Christian hymn I learned as a young boy.

> *God sees the little sparrow fall,*
>
> *It meets His tender view;*
>
> *If God so loves the little birds,*
>
> *I know He loves me, too.*

Christianity is sentimental. It believes that there is a great God in heaven that cares deeply about what happens to each and every human being that has ever lived. The Christian universe is supposed to be humane.

The question is, which point of view makes the most sense?

....

80

Shortly after the terror attacks at the World Trade Centre I was invited to take part in a panel discussion at a private school. There were a lot of people present---a Cabinet minister, a representative of the Israeli government, a Roman Catholic priest, etc. I was appalled by the way these "responsible", "mainstream" people acted. To a one, they expressed an extremely emotional, freaked-out response to the 9/11 massacre. There was no attempt to try and put any of it into a context, to suggest that we shouldn't stumble around like enraged bears---creating more violence and evil in the world. I was the lone voice trying to put the attacks into an objective perspective in order to calm people's emotions. I said that bad as the attack was, the casualties would have been considered a quiet day in WWII---which went on for about six years! I also said that we have to remember that each and everyone of us is going to die and that we shouldn't be so emotionally freaked out by something like this. I ended by reading out the above passage from the Laozi.

I've spent a lot of time thinking about that event as I watch the horrors that have been inflicted on the world by the catastrophic invasion of Iraq and the never-ending "war on terror". Why was I the only voice suggesting moderation? I would suggest that it is because these other people were working through a false understanding of life. They believed in the words of that child's hymn that I learned at Sunday school. They literally believed that "Jesus loves them".

Of course, none of them would parrot that little song. Some of them weren't even nominal Christians. But I suspect that if you pressed them, they would all have ultimately come up with some expression that the universe is, or at least in some metaphysical ways should be, "fair". The emotional response that these "leaders" all manifested came from the cognitive dissonance that stomped with leaden feet into their lives on 9/11. The world isn't "fair"---your day can start with a proper breakfast, you can kiss your spouse, you can line up all your career "ducks in a row", and out of nowhere some lunatic will fly an airplane into your building and incinerate you with jet fuel.

Have a nice day!

....

For Laozi it isn't just that you can have everything going for you and if you are unlucky bad things happen. No, it's worse than that, it is inevitable that bad things happen. Look at the second stanza of Chapter Five:

"Between heaven and earth,

How like a bellows (t'o yo) it is!"

Who exists between heaven and earth? People do! And where is a bellows used? In the forge of a blacksmith. Laozi is suggesting that people's lives are like the fuel in a blacksmith's forge. We are one of the raw materials of existence that gets burned up and consumed in the Dao process. This analogy fits perfectly as straw dogs get burned in a fire during the ritual they serve. And, as I told those school children, whether or not you get crushed, incinerated, or, jump to your death during a terrorist attack---you are still going to die no matter what. Indeed, while I was saying this, my eyes focused on a bald little boy who I suspected had cancer and was going through chemo therapy. How is dying of terminal cancer better than being smashed by a bunch of Islamo-Fascists?

We are all straw dogs.

And yet, there is a little bit of an answer to the bleakness of this passage.

"Empty and yet inexhaustible,

Moving and yet it pours out ever more."

The Dao exists and maybe it has a purpose even if it is indifferent to our personal desires. It is possible to build a life where one actually puts an ideal ahead of yourself---even if many people think that this is completely impossible. Stoics used to believe that "Virtue is its own reward". This credo says that you don't "do the right thing" because you expect a reward---even if it is just a good feeling about yourself---but simply because it is the thing to do. In same way, I understand that pre-Christian Norsemen believed that courage was an ultimate virtue. You weren't courageous because it would make you a great warrior, but just because it was inherently the thing to be. Scientists also derive real meaning and purpose in their lives simply based on the quest for knowledge---not so they can patent some invention and make money or get a Nobel prize---but just because it is the thing to do. In much the same way, Daoists identify and appreciate the amazing process of existence that constantly transforms everything---plants, animals, rocks, people, energy, etc---into something else. Even strawdogs give off smoke and ashes that feed the plants, and, heat to warm the hands. For Daoists that is enough.

The Frog in the Well

Donald Rumsfeld is famous for saying that there are "things we know, things we know that we don't know, and, things that we don't know that we don't know". As a general principle this is quite true. In his case, however, I think it's fair to say that he is speaking in "bad faith" because he is an example of someone who refuses to interact with, let alone listen to, anyone who would try to expose him to something he "doesn't know that he doesn't know". In his case the "unknown unknowns" multiplied because of his arrogance.

In contrast, Daoists try to remind themselves that there are "unknown unknowns". One of the ways they do this is by thinking about a famous passage from the Zhuangzi. In the chapter identified as "Autumn Floods" a character named Kungsun Lung complains to a prince Mou that he has a hard time understanding master Chuang (Zhuangzi.) Mou explains why this is by talking about a frog that lives in a broken-down well and its conversation with a sea turtle.

> *---'I really enjoy myself here!' it said to a turtle of the Eastern Sea. 'If I want to go out, I jump along the railing around the well, then I come back and rest where the brick lining is missing from the wall. I enter the water till it comes up to my armpits and supports my chin. When I slop through the mud, it covers my feet and buries my toes. Turning around, I see crayfish and tadpoles, but none of them is a match for me. Furthermore, I have sole possession of all the water in this hole and straddle all the joy in this broken-down well. This is the ultimate! Why don't you drop in some time, sir, and see for yourself?'*

"But before the turtle of the Eastern Sea could get his left foot in, his right knee had already gotten stuck. After extricating himself, he withdrew a little and told the frog about the sea, saying, 'A distance of a thousand tricents is insufficient to span its breadth: height of a thousand fathoms is insufficient to plumb its depth. During Yü's time, there were floods nine years out of ten, but the water in it did not appreciably increase; during T'ang's time, there were droughts seven years out of eight, but the extent of its shores did not appreciably decrease. Hence, not to shift or change with time, not to advance or recede regardless of amount---this is the great joy of the Eastern Sea.' Upon hearing this, the frog in the broken-down well was so utter startled that it lost itself in bewilderment.

Zhuangzi, (Wandering on the Way, "Autumn Floods"), Mair translator.

The frog simply cannot understand what it is like to live as a sea turtle in the vastness of the ocean. Moreover, as someone who's lived his whole life in a well, he can't even know that the ocean exists. The only thing that he can possibly do is embrace some form of intellectual humility and realize theoretically that there are limits to his understanding and stay open to the possibility that something will come totally "out of left field" and surprise him. That's part of the Daoist response to life. How sad that important leaders of great nations often have not learned the same lesson!

The Three Treasures

In Chapter 67 of the Dao De Jing we are introduced to the "three treasures".

2. I have three treasures (pao),

To hold and to keep:

84

The first is motherly love (tz'u),

The second is frugality (chien),

The third is daring not be at the world's front.

3. With motherly love one can be courageous,

With frugality one can be wide reaching,

Daring not be at the world's front,

One can grow to a full vessel (ch'i).

4. Now to discard motherly love, yet to be courageous,

To discard frugality, yet to be wide reaching,

To discard staying behind, yet to be at the front,

One dies!

5 One with motherly love is victorious in battle,

Invulnerable in defense.

When Heaven wills to save a people,

It guards them with motherly love.

Ellen Chen, trans.

The three treasures of Daoism are something like the ten commandments and "golden rule" rolled up into one. But to a modern Western ear they sound bizarre and paradoxical. How can "motherly love" help you win battles? How does frugality help anyone become "wide reaching"? And how does one dare not to be at the "world's front"?

Motherly Love

When we go hiking in the wilderness one thing that everyone knows is that you should try to never get in between a mother and her child. Not only does this apply to ferocious predators like wolves, bears and cougars, but also normally peaceful animals like moose or even deer. This is because mother animals protecting their young have a fearlessness and ferocity that is unmatched. Predators chasing prey are wary of being injured. As are males fighting over potential mates. But mothers don't care about their own safety at all.

The other aspect of this to remember is the immunity that mother animals have towards retaliation. If an animal attacks humans as prey or because it is too "familiar" with human beings, game wardens will hunt it down and kill it as a matter of course. But if the attack came from someone getting in between mother and cubs, generally people acknowledge that there was no blame, except perhaps on the part of the human. I have read accounts by people who were lying in hospital beds after savage maulings that show the same sentiment.

In the relations between people and nations it is a sad fact of existence that violence is sometimes necessary. But Daoists try to always act with the love of a mother towards her children. That means when it is necessary, they need to fight to both ferociously and fearlessly. But the act of violence needs to be directed towards only one aim: defense. All violence must be proportionate and directed specifically towards whomever or whatever is the threat. And once the threat is passed there is absolutely no room for animosity or grudges.

We have recently had many examples of what happens when one doesn't follow this principle. Wars that are not about defense but rather about the "interests" of states have severely damaged those same interests. And wars that were based on "shock and awe" and which accepted far too much "collateral damage" have created violent responses by people enraged by the carnage they have seen inflicted on their communities. As long as a nation restricts its military activity

86

to genuine defense, it has the respect of the world. But once it embarks on needless adventures it becomes a pariah.

Exactly the same thing happens in our personal lives. We all have boundaries that we need to defend: personally, in our family, and, in the various communities we inhabit. This means that conflict is pretty much inevitable at least once in a while. But Daoists believe that the best way to manage them is by remembering to keep the ideal of the love between a mother and her child as the guiding principle that informs our actions and responses. Of course, no one can ever live totally according any ideal. But it is what we strive towards.

....

Another way of looking at this passage is to consider the quality of the relationships one builds in society and how that affects one's influence within it. Another book strongly influenced by the Daoist viewpoint is Sun Tzu's **Art of War**. Consider this passage:

> *A general regards his men as infants who will*
> *march with him into the deepest valleys. He treats*
> *them as his own beloved sons and they will stand by*
> *him unto death. If a general indulges his men but is*
> *unable to employ them, if he loves them but cannot*
> *enforce his commands, if the men are disorderly*
> *and he is unable to control them, they may be*
> *compared to spoiled children, and are useless.*

(Chapter 10, General Tao Hanzhang version, Yuan Shibing trans.)

This idea of a parent sending her children off to fight a war may grate on some people's ears. But the important issue is how the general feels towards her men. Sun Tzu's general is genuinely concerned about her soldiers. She doesn't see them as a means to an end, or, as pawns to move on a chess board in order to advance her career or to prove some aspect of a pet ideology. They are subjects, not objects.

Having said that, it is important to remember that a Daoist is not just any type of mother, she is someone who acts in a certain way. That is to say, she is not sentimental. This means that while she treats her soldiers like her own children, she is the type of mother that is not indulgent. She believes in "tough love". Being overly indulgent towards your children is another form of objectification. This is because the sentimental mother doesn't see her children as individuals that have their own agendas and need to find their own way in the world, but rather as puppets that act out the emotions that dominate her consciousness. Objectively viewing your children as human beings in their own right instead of extensions of your internal mental state can be a profound act of love towards them.

If we treat our children as being autonomous individuals who have rights beyond what we want them to be, then they also have responsibilities too. And we expect those children to live up to those responsibilities. Soldiers do not respect officers who over-indulge them because the smart ones realize that their welfare is bound up with the group. Sailors say a "tight [ie: well-disciplined] ship is a happy ship". This is because in a slack ship the best men end up doing extra work that the worst ones shirk. And wise ancient Roman soldiers said "slack officers lose battles". And, there can be no greater calamity for a soldier than losing a battle.

This point is reinforced by what immediately precedes the above quote from Sun Tzu:

> *---the general who in advancing does not seek*
> *personal fame, and in retreating is not concerned*
> *with disgrace, but whose only purpose is to protect*
> *the country and promote the best interests of his*
> *sovereign, is the precious jewel of the state.*

(Chapter 10, General Tao Hanzhang version, Yuan Shibing trans.)

The General who acts according to Daoist principles is selfless. She doesn't care about her career. She isn't dominated by whatever emotional baggage she might be carrying. She is like the mother cougar or grizzly who defends her cubs without any thought to her self interest. It is the same for the Daoist in society---only the "off-spring" may be many things. It may be the soldiers under her command, it may be the sovereign she serves, or, it may be the greater good of the entire community. Unfortunately, these sorts of leaders are very rare, which is why the competent sovereign needs to treat them like "the precious jewel of the state".

Frugality

Daoists are not opposed to nice things, but they would argue that most come with some sort of cost. And it is important to be aware of that cost in advance to avoid paying too high a price. What this means is that the frugal man has fewer entanglements that limit his freedom. For example, someone who is living pay-cheque to pay-cheque is less likely to quit his job when his boss starts to pressure him to do something immoral. Similarly, he will have less money to offer to charity or a friend in need. Being "wide reaching" means thinking about more than the day-to-day grind. Being over-committed narrows that focus.

And being "frugal" isn't just about money. Time can also be something that we "over commit". The conflict between family time and career has become such a commonly recognized problem that there is a bureaucratic title for the issue: "work/life balance". Books have been written and consultants are hired to give seminars. The person who has developed a career that is too time intensive will find that she no longer has the freedom to love her partner, be a parent, or, have any real friends.

Just as importantly, she will also find that she no longer has time to be open to new ideas and spontaneous in her actions. Over-committed women do not read books on subjects they know nothing about. Nor do they meet people who live totally outside her class, family, or professional orbit. This means that she effectively stops learning. Again, there is a bureaucratic name for this phenomenon: living in a "silo".

Think about the problem from the viewpoint of computer science. The power of a computer resides in its "RAM". This is an acronym that stands for "Randomly Accessible Memory". A computer with a lot of RAM is able to access and connect bits of information from a lot of different sources at the same time. In the same way, a person who has "wide ranging" interests and knowledge about society can make connections and see patterns that do not appear to people who specialize on what is important to their profession to the exclusion of all else. This is why "silo" thinking is a problem for large institutions. To give one example, if all the senior executives at your telephone company are focused on improving the ability of the existing system to provide long distance phone calls, they might not realize that there are new start up companies that are developing Voice Over Internet Phone (VOIP) technology (e.g. Skype) that completely bypasses the phone company's long distance billing system. They may also not notice an entire emerging generation of people who would rather type out chat messages than make voice-based phone calls.

Beyond the issue of money and time, there is another one: "loyalty". People build their lives around allegiances to specific notions or ideals. These can include various concepts like "the Law", "Free Enterprise", "a Good Job", "the Church", "the Party", and so on. There's the stock image of the failed party official or general who "takes the easy way out" by blowing his brains out with a revolver. We also have an iconic image of failed investors jumping to their death after a stock market plunge has "wiped them out". Below the level of suicide, we have individuals who are so emotionally invested in an institution that they progressively find themselves committing greater and greater moral outrages in order to prop it up. One example of this is the Catholic Church's desperate attempts to protect pedophile clergy.

People who have signed-up to institutions that require this commitment often pay a steep price for being "wide ranging" in their viewpoint. Chelsea Manning is in prison because she felt that people needed to see what sort of horrible outrages were being committed by the US military in Iraq. Edward Snowden is an exile in Russia because he felt that the citizens of the world needed to know how comprehensively intelligence agencies were spying on them. And, Julian Assange is a prisoner in the Ecuadorian embassy because he created the institution, Wikileaks, that allowed both Manning and Snowden to expose their information to the wider world. Whistle blowers are prime examples of people who have not been frugal in swearing personal allegiance and paid a big price for being "wide ranging". (It might be, however, that they pay less of a price than those who simply "go along" with the institutions they serve and as a result destroy their innate sense of right and wrong. There are worse places to be than prison.)

··········

Beyond these obvious issues, Ellen Chen's commentary on this section of the ***Tao Te Ching*** talks of resonances in the original ancient Chinese of the word that we translate as "frugality": "Chien is organically connected with p'u, the original state of nature as the uncarved wood. Chien stands for the economy of nature that does not waste anything."

This is somewhat similar to the relationship between the words "economy" and "ecology". They are joined together by the "eco" which comes from the Greek word "oikos", or "household". "Eco" about where we live. And the "logy" comes from "logos", or the various ways we try to articulate or understand a specific aspect of life. In this sense "oikos" plus "logos" means "understanding where we live". The "nomy" of "economy" comes from the word "nemein", or "to distribute". So "oikos" plus "nemein" means "distributing what our home has". For the Daoist what we call "frugality" doesn't just entail the money we save in our bank account, but also how lightly we walk upon the earth. And this doesn't mean "doing without", so much as being integrated into the economy of nature where nothing is wasted and everything is recycled.

Because the Daoist has worked his way into the warp and weave of his surroundings, he is able to do things that would be impossible if he were wasting resources battling with his environs. The joke that says "When you are up to ass in alligators it is hard to remember that you are here to drain a swamp" makes no sense to a Daoist. This is because in most cases he wouldn't see why the swamp should be drained in the first place. And if he did have to do something about it, he probably would find some way of doing so that wouldn't entail causing problems for the large reptiles.

············

Yet another way to think about this is to consider frugality in terms of "economy of design". Consider the 19th century American sect called the "Shakers". They had an aesthetic that was based on the simplicity and frugality that is very much in keeping with Daoist principles. Aaron Copeland made one of their hymns famous by putting it in his score for Martha Graham's ballet "Appalachian Spring". The lyrics could have come from a Daoist text:

'Tis the gift to be simple, 'tis the gift to be free

'Tis the gift to come down where we ought to be,

And when we find ourselves in the place just right,

'Twill be in the valley of love and delight.

When true simplicity is gained,

To bow and to bend we shan't be ashamed,

To turn, turn will be our delight,

Till by turning, turning we come 'round right.

The Shakers were also famous for their furniture design, which was based on a lack of ornamentation plus utilitarian design. One of their ideas, for example, was to design chairs that could easily be hung on the wall when not in use, which allowed a room to be "re-purposed" for another task, such as dancing. (The Shakers were big into dancing, hence the "turn, turn" and "turning, turning"---which are dance instructions in the above lyrics.)

I'm belabouring the issue of frugality because our society seems to have lost the ability to incorporate economy into design. Instead of cooling our homes by having windows that open and catch a breeze or using shade to avoid the hot sun, we build expensive air conditioning systems that eat huge amounts of electricity. And instead of designing cities in ways that encourage people to use transit, bicycle, or walk to work---planners create sprawling subdivisions where every adult has to own their own automobile. We also create needlessly complex systems of governance that necessitate the creation of armies of non-productive "experts" who consume society's resources---lawyers, managers, prison guards, social workers, tax accountants, bureaucrats, etc. Economists have a phrase to identify this sort of "anti-frugal" design: "enforced scarcity". That is, the creation of an environment so profoundly inefficient that people are forced to make an artificially high income in order to simply survive. This is why it is that even though we are the richest society the world has ever seen yet we still have beggars on the street and the government says it cannot afford to deal with them or any other major social problem.

Daring to Not Be at the Front of the World

One of the things that institutes of higher education usually describe as "part of their mandate" is to teach young people something called "leadership". I've often wondered why they do that. Why not teach "citizenship" instead? Actually, I suspect that most of us are a little wary of people who just assume that they should be the "leader". Why them? Why shouldn't they be "followers"? Indeed, do we really need to have "leaders" and "followers" at all? Why not have a system of equality where everyone co-operates? Even if we accept that it is necessary to divide the human population into "leaders" and "followers", then how do we decide which is which?

But if we accept that there are difficulties with "leadership", that doesn't explain why it is that a Daoist should "dare not to be at the front of the world". To understand this, look at what the DDJ says is wrong with it. "Daring not to be at the world's front, One can grow to a full vessel", and, "To discard staying behind, yet to be at the front, One dies!".

In some situations it can be a very bad thing to be visible. In the West there is something called "the tall poppy syndrome". According to Wikipedia, it comes from a passage in Herodotus' **The Histories** where a ruler asks for advice about how to govern a city. The advice is given by a person who walks through a wheat field and breaks off all the heads that have grown higher than the average. The implication is that anyone in the city who shows exceptional ability---and is therefore a potential leader of any future opposition---should be killed. The Japanese have an aphorism that says much the same thing, "A stake that sticks out will be hammered". Which is to say, anyone who makes themselves visible by being better than the herd will end up being beaten down to conformity.

China has never been a liberal democracy, which means that pretty much from the time when the **_Tao Te Ching_** was first created until present days, "standing out in the crowd" has been a dangerous thing to do. In fact, I can remember having a conversation about this with a roomie from Shanghai who said that the best strategy in life is to be "useful" without being "threatening". People get executed or assassinated in purges when they support one side and the other wins. Or, even if they just "get in the way" of another person's personal ambitions. Keeping your head down and being invisible can be life-saving advice.

Even if you aren't living in a piranha tank, it can pay to avoid putting yourself in front. There are a lot of very competitive places of work where anyone who aspires to upper management is putting themselves in for a big risk. Where I work, for example, managers have none of the official job security that the unionized employees have.

....

Beyond this very obvious issue of "life or death", there is another way of looking at this issue. Being able to "grow to a full vessel" has a double meaning that is missed by modern people. In ancient China minor infractions of the law involved amputation. If you made a mistake you would have a piece of your "vessel" cut off. (Just like Japanese Mafia members who have fingers cut off for minor mistakes.) But once we recognise this literal meaning, a metaphor becomes obvious---there is a psychological "vessel" too.

Being "in front" is a social role that requires a certain type of psychological make-up to sustain. For example, "humility" is usually considered a virtue, yet it is a vice for leaders. Leaders have to constantly blow their own horn in order to get ahead. A leader who quietly works behind the scenes will never get noticed, and therefore will never get promoted. Similarly, any leader that admits her mistakes or always tries to give credit where it is due will be seen as "weak". In addition, leaders have to be enormously disciplined with both their attention and time in order pursue their goals---this stifles creativity and keeps them from learning unexpected information.

The problem with deciding to blow your own horn and never admit errors, of course, is that pretence eventual turns into belief. Play the role of the infallible leader long enough, and you will start to believe your own propaganda. And, if a person stops admitting to himself that he makes mistakes, he loses the opportunity to learn from that particular experience. Moreover, once a leader stops believing in the possibility of making mistakes, she eventually surrounds herself with "yes men" who remove the possibility of even learning about---yet alone from---mistakes. This is why so many leaders seem to constantly make the same mistakes over and over again in their careers.

In the same way, if someone never gives credit to others for her successes, she will soon find herself surrounded by second-rate people. Partially this is because no one wants to have the value of their work ignored. But more importantly, if you don't publicly acknowledge a person's worth, eventually you won't do so privately either. And once this happens, the leader will only be interested in the advice of people who agree with him. This is why leaders often start out with great lieutenants and end up surrounded by nonentities.

I used to be appalled by the number of national leaders who set out at a very early age to become the President (eg Bill Clinton) or Prime minister (eg Brian Mulroney) and then devoted all their energies to that goal. I still find it sad, but now I expect it. The "collateral damage" must be appalling---how many people devote all their energies to a goal like this yet end up falling to the wayside for one reason or another? Even if a person does succeed, how many opportunities to learn and grow as a human being are sacrificed to the all-absorbing long term goal? This is why leaders often seem so tremendously isolated from the rest of society. Think about the people who led the US into the war in Iraq. When interviewed many of them opine that "hindsight is 20/20" and "who knew that we would get into so many problems?" Well, the head of the US army, Eric Shinseki, for one---who was forced into early retirement when he warned that far too few troops were being sent. As did the hundreds of thousands---if not millions---of people all over the world who protested against the invasion. How can people like Dick Cheney and Donald Rumsfeld be so obtuse? A Daoist could ask "how could they not?". The process that led to their gaining their positions of great influence and power mitigated against them ever being sensitive to the information that was immediately obvious to most other people.

Cloudwalking Owl (Bill Hulet) has done a lot of things. He started out in a peasant family in rural Ontario. As a young adult, he went to university and eventually got a Master's degree in philosophy. He has worked at a variety of menial jobs, ending up as a porter in an academic library. On the side, he's been involved in many different projects including helping write the constitutions of a couple political parties, organizing and managing a local currency system, bioregional congresses, a rent strike, a "free university", a municipal political party. He's also run for public office several times, at all three levels of governance. In addition he has done a fair amount free-lance writing, did a weekly column for the local newspaper, and, sued Walmart on behalf of a coalition of local clergy. Currently, he has just started an on-line magazine devoted to municipal issues in his home community of Guelph, Ontario. (See "The Guelph Back-Grounder".)

As mentioned in the book, he was also initiated into a school of Daoism and has spent most of his life learning how to live a life in harmony with the Dao. He has published on this subject for many years at his blog "Diary of a Daoist Hermit".

He has also published another book titled, ***Walking the Talk: Engaging the Public to Build a Sustainable World***. It is available as an ebook through Smashwords and other retailers, plus as a hard copy through Lulu Books. Primarily, it deals with the interface between spiritual and environmental issues.

....

If you enjoyed this book, please consider writing a review on the website where you purchased it. Self-publishing only works if people "spread the word" about books that they found entertaining.